The

DOLPHIN

and the

TORTOISE

How **SELF-AWARENESS** *impacts*
AGILE TRANSFORMATIONS

The

DOLPHIN

and the

TORTOISE

Jason Wrubel

Printed in the United States of America.
Library of Congress Control Number: 2019908059
ISBN: 978-1-949639-93-3

Cover Design: Melanie Cloth
Layout Design: George Stevens

To my children, Ariel and Jake.
I've always wanted to explain what I do and
thought writing a book was a good start.

Contents

About the Author

Jason Wrubel drives large-scale agile transformations for public and private companies across industries. Jason combines the foundational skills he has developed over the last twenty years working at traditional consulting firms with the operational and technology experience he gained from start-up roles at fast-growing organizations. His start-up exposure cultivated a deep interest in organizational effectiveness and the process behind building and scaling high-performance organizations. He enjoys working with a range of large and small companies to drive the delivery of value to their customers with greater speed, efficiency, and predictability.

Jason is the founder of Wrubel Consulting. He grew up in New York in a family of entrepreneurs and with a learner's mindset which led him to study economics, history, and business at the University of North Carolina at Chapel Hill. He currently lives in New York City with his wife, son, and daughter.

Acknowledgments

This book has been several years in the making, and I owe a lot of gratitude to the many people who have helped make it a reality, both directly and indirectly. First and foremost, I'd like to thank my wife, Michelle, for her love, support, unending patience, and for continually pushing me to write this book. To Ariel and Jake, who have taught me far more than I will ever teach them. I'd like to thank my mom and dad, who instilled a love of books at a very early age. To my sister, Lauren, who helped get me through those first eighteen years. I'd like to thank my close friend and mentor, Vib Prasad, for his ongoing coaching, support, and friendship. I'd like to thank David Dowd for continually pointing out the true meaning of freedom and letting go—I'd never have written this book without our constant dialogue. Thank you, John Krewson, who taught me a great deal about the principles of agile and clever ways of presenting them. To Sunil Arora, for reviewing many of the chapters and keeping me honest both with this book and in my career. Thank you, Frank Thoennes, for pointing out a critical addition to my table of contents and then reviewing that chapter with me. I'd also like to thank Wes Moss for convincing me to write the book and pointing me in the right direction. And finally, thank you, Adam Green. There's no way this book would have happened without you.

Foreword

Change isn't easy, but it doesn't have to be difficult either! For any company considering a major transformation to a new software product development methodology such as Agile, the journey must begin with an honest and deep introspection of how you arrived at this point in your company's maturity, what goals you want to achieve through the transformation, and critically, where do you start and how do you set yourself up for success. Having an experienced guide, who has both led and consulted with companies on successful Agile transformations, is critical to achieving success and is key to *your success.* You need a guide who understands transformation requires more than just teaching developers and scrum masters the Agile methodology and its various incarnations such as Scrum. Jason Wrubel is that guide.

I had the pleasure and fortune of working directly with Jason Wrubel where he led and distributed large product, development, operations, and leadership teams through a complex and challenging Agile transformation. Jason brought his years of experience across multiple industries as a development leader, executive coach, and technologist to bear on our journey to Agile. He understands that a successful Agile transformation requires more than just focusing on teaching a new process for development teams. Jason helps you understand that in order to be successful, you need to change your entire culture and operating model by which all teams collaborate. It's not just about the processes or developers; rather it is an amalgamation of all those things combined with a cultural change and way of thinking about problems, their solutions, and customers' needs that is required to be successful.

In this book, Jason guides you through the entire journey with practical examples, anecdotes, and analogies to help you understand that the key to success requires the willing participation of the entire organization with a strong desire to change. He shows you that for any solid structure to endure, you need to design and build a solid foundation upon which to transform your organization. As Jason leads you through the journey, he doesn't jump right in with teaching "Agile 101" and Scrum or similar Agile operating models; that's the easy part! Jason takes the time in understanding the maturity of an organization: how did it get here, how do the teams integrate and work to deliver customer value, and what the culture is that permeates how it operates and informs the decisions that it makes. He further educates you on the importance of technology and the role it plays—the tools and frameworks that are needed—in order to *be Agile*.

Jason recognizes that while software development teams largely operate using common tools and frameworks and follow common Agile practices, Agile is much more than that. A successful transformation is not "copy-and-paste" from one company to the next. Each company is unique and requires an approach that recognizes this and uses it to their advantage. In other words, as Jason guides you on your organization's journey to be Agile, he helps you understand deeply what you have to build upon and how it needs to be re-factored with all stakeholders in your organization in order to support and nurture a successful transformation.

Will you follow the Dolphin or the Tortoise? Let Jason be your guide. Happy travels on your transformation!

Francis Thoennes
SVP, Business Operations

DOLPHINS AND TORTOISES

Galapagos tortoises have a lot going for them. They have one of the longest life expectancies of any animal, with some living up to 150 years. Generally, they weigh a quarter of a ton but don't require a ton of food to sustain them. Perhaps most appealing is that they're by and large impervious to harsh weather and would-be predators: their shells create an insular fort; they merely have to dig in and hide behind that tough exterior, ensuring that they'll live another day.

Dolphins also have a lot going for them. They're incredibly social creatures, not unlike humans, forging bonds with others, caring for their injured, living in groups of around twelve members, and communicating by unique verbal and nonverbal means. They can learn, they can teach, they use simple tools such as marine sponges, and significantly, they can cooperate. They have very complex social networks. Dolphins are also one of a handful of animals who are self-aware: they can see themselves in the mirror and understand what they're seeing is their own selves. This kind of self-awareness is a precursor to advanced intelligence. They use their reflections to investigate and figure things out about themselves.

Companies have to know themselves and take part in an investigative process to adapt to a new framework.

Both of these animals enjoy popularity with marine animal lovers, and both have thrived in one way or another. But if you were to bet on one of these creatures lasting far into the future with the various threats facing the seas, the climate, and their ecosystem, you probably wouldn't take the slow-moving tortoise, with its reproductive issues and placement on the endangered list. Thanks to their complex social networks, self-awareness, and adaptability, dolphins represent how a twenty-first-century company should strive to be: cooperative, communicative, and agile.

It's the self-awareness that makes the dolphins so advanced, and continually investigating. And it's the lesson that I like to impart to businesses in which I embed myself as a consultant. Companies have to know themselves and take part in an investigative process to adapt to a new framework. In order to deliver value more quickly, more predictably, and with higher quality if you're undertaking or fixing an agile transformation, you need to be self-aware enough to know where you're starting from, what your weaknesses and strengths are, how you operate, and what you want to accomplish.

When companies reach a level of growth and age, they have a tendency to dig in and entrench themselves in what seems comfortable—what they've always done. Forward-thinking organizations recognize that the landscape is continually changing and self-evaluate a lot; they communicate, intermingle, and adapt. This is all to say that if you want to succeed with your agile transformation, don't be a tortoise. Be a dolphin.

Chapter 1

A BETTER AGILE
IS CLOSER THAN
YOU THINK

Stop me if you've heard this one: Months ago, company X had agile thrust onto it by a senior executive, and in a whirlwind week and a half, an army of besuited outsiders swooped in and presented a "So You're Going Agile!" workshop, designating former project managers (PMs) as "champions," despite the fact that nobody really knew what was going on. The response was underwhelming at best. Now some team members are quietly acknowledging their frustration in the new world of agile while others are a lot more vocally expressive about it. What's more, the company that promised a big return on the investment in agile thought leaders came with a pretty hefty price tag … and yet nothing's changed.

Managers have been barking orders to software engineers, telling them how important it is to follow preexisting steps. The engineers could not care less about the transformation. Morale is down, and designers feel disconnected from the product. Retrospective meetings are actually hour-long venting and finger-pointing sessions. Upper management is concerned with metrics, and executives consider themselves separate from the entire process. Valuable work time is spent on coming up with story names and templates, people are drowning in burn-down charts, and the 850 scrum rules are getting on everyone's very last nerves.

If any of these obstacles sound familiar, don't worry. You're not alone. While agile is an incredibly useful and productive approach for our day and age, it's being implemented poorly—and in many cases flat-out incorrectly—at businesses across the world. In fact, often, the main beneficiary of an agile implementation is the fancy company that set up the training schedules and doled out certifications in scrum, Nexus, LeSS, and everything in between. Unfortunately, these courses are taught in a vacuum, often in ignorance of the workplace and the people they will impact. And a two-day seminar wouldn't be able to automatically create product owners (POs) who can help transform a decades-old internal methodology. There's no one-size-fits-all approach when it comes to agile. Every situation is unique, every company is unique, and every employee is as well.

I get this question a lot: How can I, as an individual, compete with a company sporting a fifteen-person, $3 million engagement, offering quick and easy agile implementation? After all, I don't have training in product management, or software engineering, or design. I'm a guy from Westchester by way of North Carolina who thought the only way to fix the Nintendo Entertainment System (NES) gaming system was by blowing on the cartridges and furiously hitting the reset button. But corporations looking for an agile transformation are seeking out my services because they understand that what I'm preaching isn't shortcuts and easy certifications and nicknames.

My diverse background taught me that all things are about people and relationships. And managing *those* is what I became really good at through my experience working with product, software engineering, and operations teams at start-ups and Fortune 1000 companies. My added value is not in content; it's not in expertise in these technical spaces. What I bring to the table is something every company needs: an understanding of what makes people and organizations tick, and a knack for getting the most out of both.

No matter how automated tasks become, and no matter how far-flung our workforces are, any company that has employees, systems, and processes—and that's just about every company in the world—has the same needs and runs into the same roadblocks. Invariably, every company needs somebody to come in and ask the questions that have to be asked. Every company requires someone to show them how they can improve their operations, someone to be a mentor and coach, and most

Before you can replace a decades-old methodology with agile, you have to do one simple thing: know yourself.

importantly, someone who understands people and relationships.

That understanding is the *sine qua non* for instituting agile.

Before you can replace a decades-old methodology with agile, you have to do one simple thing: know yourself. That's my approach, and it's something I'll come back to. Know what your company is solving for, know how the people working for you operate, know how the executives think, know where your organization is, and know what your workplace environment is like. Let's analyze your workforce and extract the most out of them; let's craft positive and collaborative working relationships between somebody who's been coding for twenty years and a PO who doesn't know the first thing about software engineering. Let's drill down to your company's core values and quantify your culture.

That's what I do, and that's what this book will reflect.

Because so much of the internet economy is based on catching up to, and keeping up with, the Joneses, for fear of being left behind, companies are looking to adopt new technologies, policies, and structures before fully understanding *what* exactly they're bringing on. People were proselytizing about "shifting to the cloud" before executives even fully understood the implications and requirements of that shift! And over the past eight or nine years, there's been a rush by multibillion-dollar corporations with thousands of employees to implement Agile—with a capital *A*—the flashy version of it sold from a one-size-fits-all container.[1] After all, it's hot, it's popular, and since the rise of the flexible start-up, many companies are bending over backward to onboard the entire process. You can imagine the voices from above hurriedly making this decision: "Hey! Everything's changing! We should be like a start-up! We want to be agile. Cheetahs are agile, right? Let's be like cheetahs! Let's get that high-priced team to teach us the steps, let's assign a champion, do a two-day workshop, and bing-bang-boom!"

The very mention of the term *agile* may cause a pressured executive to break out in a cold sweat. But as with all well-intentioned dogma, it's not the actual principles and practice of agile that are overwhelming; it's the misunderstanding and perversion of it that

---

1   You'll notice, throughout the book, I mostly refer to agile with a lowercase *a*. This is what we talk about when we refer to the actual underlying principles that companies can adopt for a more effective and quicker workflow. Think of capital-A Agile as the crass marketing of the form. When companies don't necessarily know the principles that will make them agile, they end up implementing only the *steps toward* agile.

has led to needlessly confused people and companies.

There are numerous ways agile can be adopted poorly by your organization if you're not ready for it. It can be forced down employees' throats, leaving them frustrated. It can be shoehorned into an environment that's not conducive to change, which can lead to friction between departments. The demand for strict adherence to hundreds of rules can set the entire staff grumbling. After all, if you don't know the principles, you're a slave to the rules. That's true for the Bible, the Constitution, and yep, for agile as well.

Those companies looking to "teach" agile in a weekend intensive or on the fly are missing these essential ingredients in their blueprint, and because of that, businesses falter with rushed or poor implementations. And that's why the previously explained scenario perhaps rings some bells, and why you're reading this book.

Adopting agile for your company can have incredible benefits but requires a holistic approach, which starts with truly understanding the underlying principles. And to get the most out of this workflow philosophy, you need to understand *why* agile works, what it is, and perhaps more importantly, what it *isn't*.

We'll explore that in a second. But as we dig into this book, unpack the philosophy, and explore these principles, and as you work on knowing yourself, put your mind at ease by asking yourself if you believe that the customer knows what she wants more than you do. And do you believe that your job is to deliver value to your customer? If you do, then congratulations! You're living up to one of the *core tenets* of agile. The rest is all execution.

Chapter 2

WHAT AGILE ISN'T ... AND WHAT IT IS

A 2018 survey of almost six thousand executives, directors, and practitioners in project management reported that 46 percent of completed projects at their organizations had used either an agile or hybrid agile-predictive approach over the prior twelve months. Additionally, 80 percent of federal operations and technology projects in 2017 were described as either "agile" or "iterative."[2] Not surprising, considering the benefits, or that such tech powerhouses as Amazon, Google, Apple, Facebook, and Microsoft all incorporate these principles to some degree.[3]

---

2   Project Management Institute, *Success in Disruptive Times,* Pulse of the Profession Tenth Global Project Management Survey 2018, accessed August 30, 2018, https://www.pmi.org/-/media/pmi/documents/public/pdf/learning/thought-leadership/pulse/pulse-of-the-profession-2018.pdf.

3   Steve Denning, "Why Agile Is Eating the World." *Forbes,* January 2, 2018, accessed August 30, 2018, https://www.forbes.com/sites/stevedenning/2018/01/02/why-agile-is-eating-the-world%E2%80%8B%E2%80%8B/

But despite its increasing popularity, misinformation persists.

Maybe you've heard some myths about agile: There's no commitment to dates, there's no documentation. It's just about making software engineers code quicker. It's only relevant to software engineering. There's no planning. It's undisciplined. It's just a new fad.

Agile was a direct response to the changing landscape of product development in a world with quicker business cycles and the need for more flexibility and less arcane, less rigid practices.

These assertions are simply not true. But how did they come to hold such sway?

From bad experiences, possibly. Any organization that believes those fabrications isn't benefitting from a correct agile implementation. Or maybe it's the fear of committing to something fundamentally different from what we're used to. Change, after all, is hard.

But agile didn't come about in a vacuum for the sake of shaking things up. It was a direct response to the changing landscape of product development in a world with quicker business cycles and the need for more flexibility and less arcane, less rigid practices.

For much of the twentieth century, the only approach to software engineering project management was waterfall, a linear flow of work that would require a set amount of time for each phase from requirements gathering to design to development to testing to deployment. Each step could only be completed after the preceding step was done.

Think about the creation of a Chemical Bank ATM in the early

1970s. The first step was requirements gathering. Over four months, analysts figured out what their ATM ought to do, and what problems it ought to solve. The documentation stage then necessitated a series of approvals for each of these use cases. For three months, the design team took those requirements and created solutions within the schematics. Then, over the course of a seven-month development phase, the ATM was built. The brand-new, money-dispensing machine was tested for a few months in order to make sure it was bug-free and ready for the public. Finally, a year and a half after conception, the ATM was deployed for customers on the streets of 1972 New York City.

Fifty or sixty years ago, business cycles were longer and customers' needs didn't change as rapidly, so there didn't need to be an alternative to waterfall. It was like an assembly line: one line worker finishes up a component of a widget and sends it down the belt to the next person, who can't start her job until the previous task is completed. But with the rise of computers and software engineering, there came a realization that the world was changing and this process wasn't quite right anymore.

Software engineering happens a lot quicker than manufacturing, and it's a lot more unpredictable. While the preordered inputs of steel, plastic, aluminum, and glass will lead to the output of an automobile (as fits the defined process), it's not so simple with software engineering: business priorities are constantly shifting and the technical landscape is constantly progressing. There's a complexity in code bases and uncertainty with changing requirements that makes the line "the best laid plans of mice and men often go awry" seem as if it had been written specifically for this field.

Agile is an acknowledgment that software engineering is not the same as the production of other goods. When Steve Jobs and his team put together the iPhone in 2006, they were flying blind. It was a brand-new idea and platform. They couldn't predict how long it would take to code an exact piece of software to integrate with the hardware, so the defined process, in which the same inputs, with the same process steps, should produce the same output (normal variance excepted), wasn't possible. Instead, they and other software engineers had to use the empirical process, a constant flow of transparency, inspection, and adaptation:

- **Transparency**: keeping everything visible

- **Inspection**: reviewing the product and process

- **Adaptation**: continually improving the product and process

These three pillars of the empirical process highlight the fact that it's impossible to bat 1.000 when developing software. The defined process and waterfall are great for manufacturing goods, but for the unpredictability of software engineering, the dynamism and malleability of the empirical process and agile approach is far superior.

Put another way, if *building* an F16 is the predictability of goods manufacturing, with the same input and the same process leading to the same output, then *flying* an F16 is the unpredictability of software engineering, needing to account for variables such as weather changes and flocks of pesky seagulls.

So in 2001, a group of seventeen practitioners met at a snowy Utah ski resort to propose lighter alternatives to the heavier, document-driven, waterfall method. Eschewing archaic traditional practices, this group wanted to highlight the importance of a model based on collaboration, and on actual community within organizations. There's nothing particularly revolutionary about that. They simply stated their core mission: to deliver quality products to customers and recognize the importance of people.

This mission became the Manifesto for Agile Software Development (below), the first effort to address the calcified bureaucracy of the old way.

> We are uncovering better ways of developing
> software by doing it and helping others do it.
> Through this work we have come to value:
>
> - **Individuals and interactions** over processes and tools
> - **Working software** over comprehensive documentation
> - **Customer collaboration** over contract negotiation
> - **Responding to change** over following a plan
>
> That is, while there is value in the items on
> the right, we value the items on the left more.

Everything you truly need to know about being agile is contained in there: How it prizes people and face-to-face interaction; how the deployment of the product trumps onerous documentation; how collaboration is key; and how change is bound to happen.

An eighteen-month linear waterfall project-management approach just isn't feasible in an ever-evolving technical landscape. Getting product changes approved in waterfall was difficult; knowing all the upfront requirements is a near-impossibility; and waiting a year and a half to roll something out to the customer doesn't make good business sense.

Over three days in that ski lodge, the group produced not just the manifesto but also twelve principles (see the appendix), each of which underscores those points. There's nothing heretical in there, and certainly nothing that software engineers or executives would disagree with. They not only debunk the myths about agile but can also show how close your mind-set already is. These principles are worth revisiting for anybody in a leadership position looking to implement agile within an organization. Is your company continuing to follow the tenets set down? Is your company valuing people and face-to-face-interaction? Is it prioritizing working software, collaboration, and iterative deployment?

Like all good teachings, the manifesto became popular, and with that popularity came bad implementation, and before long, erroneous notions about the approach.

Right off the bat, one of the most utilized methodologies for agile was scrum.[4] Innumerable books have been written about scrum, and there is likewise a monsoon of coaches and certified scrum masters. But with its ubiquity as a methodology, scrum somehow became synonymous with agile—and that's the first myth.

MYTH 1. SCRUM = AGILE.

Agile is a software engineering philosophy based on iterative engineering and focused on customer delivery. Scrum is just one *framework* for

---

4 Scrum takes its name from a 1986 *Harvard Business Review* article on product development, in which the authors used the example of a rugby scrum formation to promote the idea of small, cross-functional teams working in strong collaboration to produce the best results; they contrasted this style with the old approach, which was similar to a relay race.

bringing it about. There are many others: SAFe, XP, kanban, crystal, and dynamic systems development method (DSDM), to name a few. To equate the methodology of scrum with the approach of agile is to equate just one example with the overarching philosophy.

An analogous misunderstanding would be believing that Michael Lewis's *Moneyball*, a book detailing how baseball's Oakland Athletics found undervalued players through the use of advanced statistics, was *only* about on-base percentage (OBP), the main example cited. OBP—a stat reflecting how often a batter gets on base—was largely disregarded through the 1990s. The small-market Athletics succeeded by signing cheap players with good OBPs.

But the message of *Moneyball* wasn't about only this example, and those who thought it was missed the larger picture. It's about the approach. Almost two decades later, in 2018, the Oakland As were at it again. This time they ignored OBP and, instead, found bargains by targeting and developing players who relied on a higher "launch angle" to hit the ball in the air more often, again finding value where other teams saw none.

But just as so many came to reduce that book to following the instructions to "get a bunch of guys with high OBPs," it's easy to turn around and say, "Okay, we want agile, so let's get a scrum coach and follow these 850 particular steps."

Nope. Not that easy. If you miss the message, you miss the meaning.

Scrum has been around for a long time, but it's only one of several methodologies. A scrum team, consisting of around seven people—a PO, a scrum master, and a few team members—goes through certain iteration planning meetings to figure what items can be done in a short amount of allotted time, or iteration. Along each iteration, the team meets in a daily stand-up (or daily scrum) to determine what work each member has finished, what they plan to work on, and what's blocking them from completing that work. At the end of each iteration, the team has a review, in which they discuss what they worked on, and do a demo of the product to determine whether it's deployable. The final meeting in each time box is the iteration retrospective, in which team members reflect on the previous iteration, discussing how the process went and what could have been improved.

Scrum was originally adopted by small companies, but as larger ones recognized the need for the flexibility and quick decision-making of a start-up, they, too, were attracted to it. However, that kind of scalability wasn't available immediately with the framework, and simply following the instructions resulted in a lot of broken agile implementations. This reflects a lack of understanding of the agile manifesto, the levers and principles that distinguish software engineering from the defined process. And with no understanding of the broader concepts, these experiences engender misconceptions about what agile truly is.

So let's put some more of these prevalent myths to bed.

MYTH 2. THERE'S NO COMMITMENT TO DATES.

How many times have you heard this: Once a company transitions to agile, there won't be any dates for deliverables, software engineers will be vague with commitments, and stakeholders will be left in the dark.

That's flat-out wrong. Nowhere in the manifesto or principles does it say that agile can't abide by dates. Commitments need to happen; companies owe it to their customers and to their stakeholders. But where the flexibility comes in is the complexity and specificity of the long-term deliverable: the *scope* part of the old project management triangle, whose three sides are budget, time, and scope. In an agile process, commitment to dates works if the scope can be that flexibility lever. Ongoing planning is inherent in agile processes because we need to allow change to occur.

At the same time, because there's more predictable, iterative deployment of products and features along the way, specific scope definition is easier in the shorter term.

Think about it this way: An international bank wants to overhaul the entire login experience for a user. An agile approach allows software engineers to say with certainty and specificity that two weeks from now, customers will be able to view their account balances in blue in the top left corner of their home page.

The engineers are *also* able to commit to the entire overhaul of the system within eighteen months. But the details of what the system will provide are a lot more general a year and a half out, and as a result, the documentation is a lot lighter long before the ultimate delivery. Yes, we know that the user's home page will have some sort of statement download functionality; yes, we know that it will also be able to have some sort of transfer functionality; but the specifics will be worked out and most likely altered over the course of the long road ahead.

This is part of the acknowledgment of the unpredictable landscape of software engineering: needs may change, and it would be useless to waste hours of work documenting things that may be either archaic or unnecessary a year in advance.

So, can we commit to dates? Absolutely. But the scope is the lever.

MYTH 3. THERE'S NO DOCUMENTATION.

While it's true that agile came about partially in response to the document-heavy, waterfall, project-management approach, it would be inaccurate to say that there's no documentation. The agile manifesto simply says that the approach prizes "working software over comprehensive documentation."

In waterfall, the linear approach led to a metric ton of documentation for every requirement months before the entire system was to be delivered in a big-bang deployment. The practical result in software engineering, however, was that the project no longer became about delivering the goods but all about documenting and internal status reporting. The view of the forest was lost because of all those pesky trees. Complicated reports and documentation overshadowed the intent of the project, and focusing on the exact written rules outweighed the product itself.

The agile approach lightens that requirement for upfront documentation. Yes, it's still necessary, but less weight is given to it than to the overarching goal of working software. It also leaves room for emerging, evolving design down the road, and for teams to have creative space to tweak what needs to be tweaked along the way.

Ultimately, it's about striking a balance. Necessary and valuable documentation is always important, but needless and wasteful documentation that will end up changing anyway is a drain on resources. Figuring out which is which is key.

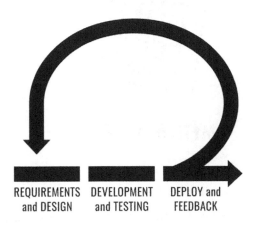

REQUIREMENTS   DEVELOPMENT   DEPLOY and
and DESIGN   and TESTING   FEEDBACK

MYTH 4. AGILE IS ABOUT MAKING SOFTWARE ENGINEERING TEAMS CODE FASTER.

This goes back to the iterative deployment idea. Instead of a linear big-bang deployment, the software engineering team has short iterations to bring constant releases to the customer. They get feedback for their "rough drafts" and adjust accordingly. This helps improve the product. It doesn't mean that they're coding faster; it just means that problems are solved in a fraction of the time it used to take.

Do solutions come *more quickly* in an agile process? Absolutely. But that's merely a byproduct of the faster lead time, not because the software engineering teams are being flogged by a taskmaster to code at hyperspeed.

But speed *never* trumps quality. Agile processes are intentionally in short bursts of deployment, but teams never sacrifice quality. Iterations ensure that rough drafts are released more often to the customers, but these always pass through proper steps of review and testing.

MYTH 5. AGILE IS NEW.

Simply reading the agile manifesto should convince you that these principles have been in play long before that Utah ski trip in 2001: Efficiently delivering value to a customer, investigating the process while remaining open to change, and eliminating wasteful practices along the way are all parts of the manifesto's underlying message. This theory has been around for hundreds of years, but for its most immediate forerunner, we can hearken back to lean manufacturing, which stemmed from the Toyota production system of the 1940s.

Looking for the most sustainable pace to deliver quality to customers is more important to the agile process than sacrificing for a slight increase in speed.

Lean is focused on optimizing efficiency and getting rid of waste to make the manufacturing workflow as smooth and continuous as possible. In order to accomplish this, bottlenecks are identified and resolved, even if that means stopping the entire production line. The reason for this short-term halt is the same as the reason for agile's short sprints and releases: it's cheaper and easier to fix a problem sooner than later in the process.

Lean and agile both ask, simply, "How do you deliver value to a customer? And how do you make that delivery as efficient as possible?"

The slight difference between the undercurrents of lean and agile is that the latter is driven more by value delivery than by optimization. Looking for the most sustainable pace to deliver quality to customers is more important to the agile process than sacrificing for a slight increase in speed. Nevertheless, to say that agile is "new" disregards this major philosophy that was in place for the post-World War II automobile manufacturing boom.

Agile Planning

MYTH 6. AGILE MEANS NO PLANNING AND NO DISCIPLINE.

This myth is part and parcel of the same mind-set: going agile means a lot of improvisation on the fly, completing tasks as you feel like it. It's the same fear-based mentality that feeds those who think that there are no commitments in agile.

Au contraire.

Just as hard-and-fast commitments are quite typically made with an agile process, detailed planning and strong discipline are both mandatory for proper implementation. Because iterative deployment happens regularly, frequent short-term planning is necessary, and because changes are not only expected but welcomed, ongoing planning is intrinsic to the process, stretches beyond the upfront work, and involves every member of the team.

And it takes a concerted amount of discipline to be agile. The short iterations, incorporating feedback into second and third drafts, consistently testing, regularly shipping software, providing retrospectives and learning, getting bad news early—all of this requires a regimented work ethic from every member of the team.

MYTH 7. AGILE IS JUST A SOFTWARE ENGINEERING THING.

This pernicious falsehood is symptomatic of a company that doesn't require commitment from everyone. The software engineering is the direct result of the agile approach, but by no means is agile meant solely for the engineering teams.

Agile requires that other teams also change how they work. It changes how they interact with the software engineers, it changes how they interface with the solution, and it changes how the entire company operates. Sales, marketing, customer service, and HR—all of these are inextricably linked to software engineering.

Take security, for example. It's housed under operations and technology, which represents both the engineering aspect (software engineering teams) as well as technical support teams (e.g., database, dev ops, biz ops, networking, and security). So even though security is not often a direct part of the software engineering team, they have to keep pace with the increased velocity of deployments and be woven into the process. Finance and accounting also need to understand the implications because of the impact on software capitalization and amortization. Software engineering accounting guidelines, by and large, have been conceived with longer-term waterfall phases. With iterative software deployment in agile, that all changes. Figuring out how (and when) to categorize software costs is mandatory for the company's finances, especially if it wants to avoid millions of dollars in SEC fines.

Agile is not just an engineering thing. It's a top-down, all-hands-on-deck thing. Software engineers may be the most involved day-to-day, but without the active support of every department *and* the executives *and* the stakeholders, a transition to agile may never come to fruition.

MYTH 8. AGILE IS A SILVER BULLET.

Transitioning to an agile approach will be greatly beneficial for your company, but it is by no means a silver bullet. Adopting agile will require holistic changes throughout the entire organization, and it all begins with my credo of know yourself, which we'll dig into in later chapters. There's no one be-all, end-all solution to problems within a company. An agile implementation can help tremendously but only if the environment is right to begin with.

Being agile doesn't make your operations and technology structure magically perfect. Implementing agile within your company isn't about following the steps of scrum or XP. It can only come about after making sure the technical environment and organizational culture are conducive to this change, the right tools are in place, and there's commitment from executives.

The consequences of changing to the agile approach will affect everyone, and it's important to internalize how much it will affect your own work within the organization. CEOs who say "Okay, agile it is! Let's spend the $10 million, and full thrusters ahead!" often overlook the fact that they'll be active participants. C-level executives will be looking at new metrics and KPIs that they're not used to. They'll have to start inspiring and visioning more than managing. Leadership won't be looking at status reports that show the project's completion percentage; there will be new ways of receiving data.

They may have to let some productive staff go if they're not fitting into the agile framework, and replace them with new blood and new skill sets.

Companies that succeed in an agile transition have learned to be both stable and flexible. They have identified who they are, what role each member plays, and what kind of environment is most conducive to high productivity. That environment demands buy-in from the entire organization to make it clear that the culture is company-wide; exceptions to the rule can be extremely harmful.

I know from experience.

I was brought into a large company that was hell-bent on becoming agile, and with my consultation, the company implemented a scaled framework in scrum and SAFe to fit its needs. As with many methodologies for agile, retrospectives were an integral part of the process. A lot of time, effort, and literal sweat and tears go into these meetings, which require participation not just from the team members but also from the executives.

For segments of three days, we assembled groups of about one hundred software engineers, testers, and other business folk from Boston, Kansas City, and Malaysia to run a very focused session through a video conference. This brought together a geographically scattered team for essential face-to-face interaction, a core tenet in agile. Some fundamental issues came up in this all-hands meeting, issues that were integral to the overall goal of delivering value to the customer. And you know what? The executives didn't show.

It's hard to blame them. The importance of their attendance had not been conveyed properly. To the executives, it looked like just another meeting on an overpacked calendar, and one that could be skipped in favor of what they thought was more critical work for the business. Had the impact of their appearance and the necessity of their attendance been accurately relayed, they would've been there. Communication is key, and something misfired along the way. As a result, the point of agile being about *everyone* in the company was nullified.

Unfortunately, team members noticed the lack of executive participation—a handful of grown men and women, senior engineers, were on the verge of tears—and you could tell in that room that the company had just lost a hundred software engineers. Right there. Because they believed they weren't heard and valued, and they believed that the organization was still beholden to a command-and-control ideology.

> Agile requires buy-in from everyone. Executives, it's not enough just to cut a check.

What I'm saying is this: agile requires buy-in from everyone. Executives, it's not enough just to cut a check. Participation is key. You have to check new metrics; you have to attend retrospective meetings because they're not just for software engineers; you may have to fire people you're comfortable with and hire new ones with different skill sets. If you're investing millions of dollars in an organizational transformation, it's incumbent on you to be part of the change. And you'll need to do it on behalf of all of your coworkers.

Everyone needs to have skin in the game. To truly be part of the collaborative effort, anyone involved in the transformation effort—executives, management, staff—should see their compensation attached to its success. If software engineers are evaluated on their application of the new approach to software engineering, it stands to reason that their bonuses, as well as those of their superiors, should also be tied to whatever outcomes have been identified for this agile transformation.

I'm not going to sugarcoat this. Agile is not easy. But the benefits are incalculable: If you approach the implementation in a holistic, top-down way, I can guarantee that you will be delivering value faster to your customers, with higher quality and more predictability. But the uncertainty and new territory will be uncomfortable for a little while.

Let's do a gut check. If this doesn't sound like something your organization can get behind—if you can't see yourself getting comfortable with this kind of responsibility—then let's stop here.

But if you are ready to fix agile within your organization, let's read on and find out what went wrong with the implementation.

Chapter 3

DID THEY RUSH THE IMPLEMENTATION OF AGILE?

As I mentioned while running down the laundry list of myths, a lot of the suspicion surrounding agile stems from fear or anxiety about how the transition will affect team members' lives and job responsibilities. It goes against the grain of the decades of command-and-control methods that they're used to. But it also may come from leadership who've had—or heard of—bad experiences or rushed implementations.

If you're still with me here, you know the benefits of an agile approach to software engineering. You know that it will result in higher quality software, with quicker deployments. That it'll create better communication within the team, bring more transparency in a field that can be confoundingly murky, remove obstacles and bottle-necks, and improve morale throughout the organization.

But you *also* know that it's tricky to get it done right. If the implementation goes badly, one, if not all, of the above benefits will be compromised, and that simply gives fuel to opponents of the transformation.

> **Rushing an agile transition is as counterproductive as telling a toddler to run before he can walk.**

Rushing an agile transition is as counterproductive as telling a toddler to run before he can walk. But that fact can be difficult to remember when an executive has green-lit an enormous check to outside consultants and expects a quick and tidy transformation into capital-*A* Agile. Executives can be beholden to shareholders and focusing on a revenue goal instead of the optimal process, or team morale can force them toward decisions that priori-tize the wrong thing because, heck, they expect results *immediately*.

It doesn't work that way.

Slapping on a this-is-how-you-agile solution, blindly following the steps of some scrum or XP or kanban framework without getting everything—the culture, the people, the tools—in place can waste those millions of dollars the executive just okayed. You rarely get a second chance at an entire workflow overhaul. So you'd better make this count.

Doing the Groundwork

I often say that while implementing large-scale, enterprise-wide agile transformations, you can't be too agile. If companies are committing to a holistic, expensive change in product management and workflow, then taking the long view with some exploration is worth it. It's not as simple as undergoing a four-month reengineering and hoping for the best. As in therapy, before you can change your behavior, you have to know what your current tendencies—good and bad—are.

I'll discuss this more in a later chapter, but I'd like you to think about the answer to this question now: What exactly are you trying to solve by transitioning? Are you adopting the agile approach simply because your competitors are? If you don't know why you're doing it, you'll have difficulty communicating the need, getting buy-in from everybody, and tailoring the transformation. Before the framework comes the groundwork. You must engage in this self-discovery, and take a good look at where *your* company is now.

And notice the emphasis on "*your* company." Every organization is different, and agile transitions for each should reflect that. This is one of the crucial elements of know yourself. Transforming your company is not a cookie-cutter procedure in which you follow preordained steps and call it a day. A start-up with forty-five people in New Haven will be drastically different from a mid-sized Raleigh outfit that started in the 1980s, which will be different from an enterprise international conglomerate based out of London.

Businesses such as Netflix, Spotify, and Tesla adopted frameworks through trial and error and landed upon tailored approaches that worked for their unique situations. They didn't copy and paste solutions from other companies, and you shouldn't either.

Before you can start applying an agile framework, it's imperative

> **As in therapy, before you can change your behavior, you have to know what your current tendencies—good and bad—are.**

to take an introspective look at your software engineering process: What are the steps associated with it? What's working? What's failing? What are the roles of each person on the team? What are the key performance indicators you use?

What a good agile transition coach can do—and this is something that I revolve my practice around—is identify team members who can describe the company's entire sequence and initiate dialogue to crystallize the company's processes and metrics.

These discussions extend beyond the rote description of the steps, though. They should serve to stitch together the overall picture of the process, and that includes what team members think is working and what's not, as well as what's preventing them from doing their job. Getting input from the people who really see the operations from the ground and figuring out how this specific organization can transform are the necessary elements. The open-ended dialogue, in which team members speak honestly about the company, suggest things they would change if they were CEO, and discuss potential obstacles to the agile transformation, reveals an awful lot. This kind of freewheeling discussion isn't limited to the engineering process alone; it should touch on every feature of the organization: the culture, the people, and even you, the leadership. Having total amnesty to speak about all aspects of the company will allow team members to fully open up.

This conversation not only helps present findings to the team and executives, but also identifies opportunities to implement agile aspects on top of the preexisting process. Just as we don't want a paint-by-the-numbers agile transformation that forces mindless directives, we also don't want to scrap all the old steps wholesale. If there are good practices, that's great. Let's figure out what those are and how we can replicate them.

Every organization has a different sense of self. Sometimes the interviews with all of the individuals involved in the software engineering process and the subsequent evaluation take several months. A hundred-step process at an organization in which each department is only vaguely aware of surrounding tasks needs a lot more piecing together. I've also worked with companies where two people know 90 percent of the process, and all it takes is a four-hour lunch with a few margaritas—well, more like two weeks.

Negotiating the entire end-to-end process of the company's software engineering and sifting through answers about the organization's inner operations seems like grunt work, but it's the first step toward a company truly knowing itself. With the number of handoffs possible along the engineering process, it's easy to allow the steps to become the focus while the overall picture falls by the wayside. The dialogue and analysis help recapture the broader picture.

Lead from What You Know

Let's say you own a pancake restaurant. The neighborhood you've faithfully served has gone carb-free, and you're reimagining the establishment as a smoothie spa. Wouldn't you want the person leading the transition to know a little something about smoothies, such as which machines blend the best, how recipes should be determined, how the kitchen should be laid out, and what kind of price tag each menu item should carry?

Since agile helps a company's software engineering process, wouldn't you want the leader for the transition to agile to have a background in software engineering? Tapping somebody from the engineering side just makes sense—a person who can visualize the payoff vis-à-vis rapidity and efficiency of product deployment, and who potentially (though not necessarily) has been there before.

Instead, what often happens in a rushed transition is that

companies simply appoint old-school project managers (PMs) who are well-versed in the traditional waterfall approach to lead the transition. They're trying to fit a square peg in a round hole because that's what the square peg does: project management. And isn't this project management?

This sometimes works. Sometimes you'll stumble upon that adaptable, open-minded senior PM who can take the training, make the switch, and lead. But more often than not, the manager—ironically the one who has to change the *most* in the new world of agile—leads the transformation through the lens of waterfall. And without underlying knowledge of software engineering and the planning cycle, the PM is going to be in way over his head. It's like the pancake maker leading the restaurant's smoothie transformation.

If you don't have the right person leading the transition, especially if the person is steeped in a waterfall point of view, the bad match can manifest itself in subconscious obstruction. Perhaps the PM will turn stand-ups into status reports because that's what he's used to, or if a PM is loyal to her organization's traditions, she may seek to bend agile requirements to fit the routine of the company, rather than the other way around.

Sometimes, however, the obstruction can be more conscious. And this can often come straight from the heads of software engineering themselves. These are people handcuffed to their approach because it's the one they've been using for twenty or thirty years. Deep down, they don't believe in agile, because it's unknown and unfamiliar, or because they recognize that they themselves will have to change fundamentally how they operate within the company. These people in leadership positions also aren't beholden to the transition; they're beholden to getting the software out to consumers by any means necessary. If they think software engineers' time is better spent in coding than in a face-to-face planning session, it's easy for them to throw up roadblocks. After all, they don't want to put their own necks on the chopping block for a workflow approach they don't believe in. So they can hedge against the transformation and pursue the end goal in the way they see fit rather than pursuing the optimal process. At least their job will be safe, even if everything else falls apart.

Tap the right person to help usher in the agile transition. Find that software engineering person, ideally with agile experience, who has skin in the game.

Train, Train, Train

It's hard for software engineering leaders indoctrinated in waterfall methodology to embrace the transition to agile and also lead it. They may feel that their roles in the organization are changing ... and they're right. Executives will have to get used to a whole new set of parameters in what they analyze and how they interact, but *every* team member will have to acclimate to new ways of doing things: new tracking tools such as Jira or Rally's ALM, new concepts, and new roles, such as scrum master and PO. How does a tester fit into the new framework? And what the heck is an agile evangelist anyway?

After the introspection, discovery, and tapping somebody to be at the helm of the transformation, the company has to commit to three different kinds of training.

- *Agile training* offers a simple primer on its concepts: dissecting the principles and explaining how each of them lends itself to making software engineering quicker and more predictable. Agile training also introduces novices to potential new roles. What's your new title, and what responsibilities and expectations come with that? Analysts becoming POs, or PMs becoming scrum masters can't expect to take on these new roles without any kind of comprehensive coaching on what that means.

Managers, in particular, will depend on that role training. After all, with the software engineers assigned a prioritized product backlog, the managers don't have to do much "managing" any more. Instead, they'll do a lot more servant-leadership: entrusting team members with responsibility, resolving conflict, removing obstacles, improving automation, and problem solving for the future.

- *Tool-based training* teaches users how to navigate the project management tools that they'll use in planning, tracking, prioritizing, estimating, and collaborating. Adjusting to using, let alone mastering, these tools can take months, or at least more than a one-hour allotment from a rushed practice session.

- *Process-based training* gives team members an idea of how to acclimate to their company's particular flavor of agile. This is helpful for getting everyone on the same page for organization-wide guidelines (such as length of iterations) or team-specific ones (such as the estimation method for sizing story points).

Don't Forget about Finance and HR

It needs to be clear from day one that training in agile won't just be for software engineers. Other departments are integral to agile's success as well. Sales and marketing need to be involved in training; they're the ones interacting with users and requesting work on their behalf. How they communicate with the product and technology teams, and how they request and track work will change. They'll be involved a bit more in meetings, and will receive different status reports. For similar reasons, customer service will need to know how product teams are changing their approach. And as seemingly uninvolved with software engineering as they are, finance and HR play critical roles and can be overlooked when agile transitions are implemented without fully thinking about the effects.

We talked briefly in the previous chapter about the implications of consistent product deployment on the accounting and finance departments. On one level, they'll have to adjust away from the old linear model in figuring out when to categorize capital expenses versus operating expenses. But a bigger concern is tracking work: Finance often dictates how work is marked and tagged in the project management tool for software capitalization purposes. It's better to know those requirements upfront, before defining the new process and rolling it out to the rest of the company without finance's input. It can be pretty deflating to see employees work hard to learn a new tracking methodology only for finance to come in two weeks later and order everyone to switch it up again.

While finance will help keep the house in order from a financial aspect, what about keeping the house in order from the personnel side? And how could HR have anything to do with being agile and improving workflow?

Consider the search for new roles. If you're looking for somebody to fit into your agile framework, seeking new hires with the job description of "project manager" is archaic and ill-fitting and will attract applicants with a different skill set from what's required of a scrum master. But again, those ensconced in the old system of waterfall and the old way of doing business may find it difficult to embrace new concepts. The old job families made sense in the old organizational structure, but now there's a new framework.

Departmental structure will change as well, and this will impact intra- as well as interdepartmental interactions. Those reporting hierarchies won't be the same anymore; with cross-functional teams and more dialogue between groups, it's likely that you'll see a shift in who's reporting to whom. Testers, for example, may not be reporting to the head of quality engineering but, rather, straight to software engineering. And that's hard for a veteran of waterfall management to get used to.

It's important to be patient with transitioning to agile.

All We Need Is a Little Patience

All of these are examples of shifting potentially resistant mind-sets to a new way of thinking. These are all part of knowing yourself and taking a step toward understanding what those guiding principles are going to be for the next iteration.

More than anything, it's important to be patient with transitioning to agile. As the Japanese poet Kobayashi Issa said,

> *"Climb Mount Fuji,*
> *O snail,*
> *but slowly, slowly."*

If it takes time and effort to accomplish something, then that's what it takes. Agile is not to be underestimated in its benefits for company earnings and team happiness, but patience is key. If your organization has rushed the transformation, chances are it's failed. Telling hundreds, if not thousands, of people who have been steeped in command-and-control hierarchy for their entire professional lives that they now have autonomy and are self-organizing may not work right out of the gate. Same thing with telling managers not to manage.

You have to start small before going big.

Often in software engineering, the pilot approach—a small rollout of the product to a select group of users for troubleshooting and feedback—can be extremely valuable. It reduces risk, improves the product, and enables better understanding of the software. And this all comes in a controlled environment, before consumers at large are privy to it.

I'm a big fan of the pilot approach for agile implementations. Instead of tackling the overall agile transition for eight hundred employees in different departments and teams, I suggest identifying a particularly strong and adaptable group on a much smaller scale. For organizations new to agile, experimenting in a contained setting like this will yield similar results as testing software with a small group of friends and family would.

In a pilot approach, a group can play with their transitioning roles to see what works. What's the best path for an analyst to become a PO? What are the philosophical changes required in making a PM a scrum master? Instead of overanalyzing things, set the transformation in progress, get feedback, and adjust accordingly—*before* implementing it company-wide.

This may be difficult for executives to understand—that for three or four months, it'll just be this crack team of thirty to forty people who will be transitioning to the agile approach. "But," they may say, "we're paying a million dollars, and we need the entire organization to be agile *now*."

Slowly, slowly, snail.

We're undoing years of waterfall methodology. It's much too important to rush implementation and see friction, obstacles, and errors on a large scale, when we could have controlled for that in a test group.

Finding a Champion

The other positive benefit of a pilot approach is that it gets a head start on identifying champions within the ranks—individuals within the small working group who can pick up the concepts early on, explain the principles, and proselytize to coworkers. As somebody who's waltzed into companies to help "fix" an agile transformation and interviewed hundreds of people from different departments, I guarantee that software engineers and other team members will respond to colleagues a lot better than they will to an external consultant (or boss, for that matter).

And that's my final warning on rushing agile implementation. If you have enlisted a consulting outfit to bring the agile principles to your organization, what happens after they leave? What does the company do if it grows exponentially? What does it do if new technology creates new requirements? You can't be dependent on outside consultants for proper agile adherence. You need in-house champions.

It may be nearly two decades since the agile manifesto was written, but the principles and concepts aren't as widely understood and appreciated as you'd think. Despite the fact that more and more companies each year are recognizing how beneficial the approach is, the core tenets are often still misinterpreted.

Outside consultants, no matter how intelligent and charming, don't have the institutional knowledge that in-house employees do. And furthermore, the transformation doesn't end when the consultant rides off into the sunset, agile six-shooters on his belt. The agile approach, as pertains to *your organization*, will be a living, breathing

thing. It'll necessarily adapt and evolve to changing realities in the business and organization, and there will have to be somebody on the ground who knows both the institution and the agile principles to help make adjustments.

By now you know that this doesn't mean finding former PMs who've been sent to a two-day certification class on scrum. This means finding those in-house champions who understand the baseline concepts and are able to answer larger-frame questions that evolve. It may mean those people sitting with the consultant for six months to see how solutions are arrived at and how agile principles are applied. As with lean, it's better to address something at a sizable cost earlier rather than later in the process, when it's both extremely difficult and extremely expensive.

The agile approach, as pertains to *your organization*, will be a living, breathing thing.

To recap, do the groundwork in figuring out the company's current approach. Identify a leader on the software engineering side who can help with the agile transformation. Get the training in place to explain the new concepts, roles, and tools and how personnel fit into the approach. Include every department, specifically finance and HR, as each will play a key part in the company's transition. Take a sample pilot team first and work on maneuvering into agile with them; discuss the positive and negative aspects, get feedback, and troubleshoot before moving to apply it to the rest of the organization. And finally, make sure you have at least one person in-house who can envision the goalposts after the consultant departs. That combination of institutional knowledge and agile comprehension will guarantee that future engineering decisions are congruous with the principles.

With all of these steps in place, from discovery to training, companies can ensure they're making the ground fertile for the transition. But to return to a question posed at the beginning of this chapter, *why* exactly are you bringing agile to your company? What are you hoping to solve? Is it simply keeping up with the Joneses (and the Musks and the Hastingses), or is there something particular you're striving for?

Answering this question is a good step in self-discovery as well, and can help build the road map for agile within your organization, as we'll see in the pages to come.

Chapter 4

COMMUNICATING THE WHY

By now we've talked about the heavy lift your company should expect if you're transitioning into an agile framework. Hey, it's more than just a couple of days of training. We're talking an overhaul in language and terminology, new systems of tracking, ignoring old metrics, examining new data points, letting go of command-and-control ideologies, pushing responsibility and accountability downward, changing personnel, and leading rather than managing.

So this is a lot to bite off. But here's a question: *Why* are you doing it? Why are you undergoing the cost, time, and personnel changes needed to adopt a new framework for your organization?

There are a lot of compelling reasons to transform. When I ask executives, I'll get a standard response: "Oh, we wanted better quality, efficiency, transparency, speed, predictability, and employee commitment." Okay, sure. Who doesn't? But think about *your* company. Why do you want your company to adopt agile specifically? What exactly are you solving for?

The Wrong Reason

Here's why *not* to adopt agile: "Everybody's doing it."

That's the excuse you give your mom when she finds a pack of cigarettes in your backpack in high school. It's not a reason for doling out a few million bucks in an agile implementation, affecting hundreds of people's jobs. Other companies may be doing it, but they have a clear vision of what agile can solve within their own business. "Because our competitor has gone agile" would be a tough sell to stakeholders when undertaking a holistic change in the way the company sees itself and operates. It's not going to help your business focus on what needs to improve, and it's not going to be a selling point for employees who have to be sold on the cost-benefit analysis.

Here's another uninspiring reason to adopt agile: "We want our software engineering team to code faster." We covered this in the myths section, but you'd be surprised by how many executives want to adopt agile as a kind of booster for software engineers. Agile doesn't automatically make any one individual do any one thing more quickly. If you're looking for that kind of solution, there are tools available to enable it. What agile does do is greatly reduce the time to market, by optimizing *everything* across the system: short iterations and constant releases enable a quicker feedback loop, with the customers' input leading to adjustments that will get the product to the right solution more quickly. But simply looking for speed is missing the forest for the trees.

So why *are* you transforming your company to an agile approach?

Because maybe agile is overkill. Maybe the problem you're looking to fix, such as simple software engineer speed, can be addressed through different means including (but not limited to) better workflow tools and embedding product and testing into the team. Maybe there are simple ingredients your organization can weave into your process without totally changing everyone's day-to-day functions. If you do implement agile, the cost in terms of people, time, money, goodwill, and short-term productivity will be real and will impact the organization. So there has to be a compelling rationale.

If you do implement agile, the cost in terms of people, time, money, goodwill, and short-term productivity will be real and will impact the organization. So there has to be a compelling rationale.

Clarity of Vision

There are two major reasons to clarify your organization's vision when transitioning to agile. First, the agile transformation road map. The intensity and focus of your training and what's most appropriate for your process will be largely based on the findings from your introspective groundwork into knowing yourself. That initial dialogue will uncover what you should be prioritizing. On a practical level, this also helps tailor an approach based on your needs. If your organization wants to, say, reduce the number of bugs in a software deployment, then we'd look at involving testers earlier in the process or exploring testing automation earlier in the transformation and with a higher focus.

The second reason the clarity of your *why* is so important is that people depend on it. The organization's leadership is going to have to explain its vision for the future to the team members. Establishing what that common goal is brings cohesion and loyalty, but it also shows respect for the hard-working employees who comprise the company.

As all those associated in software engineering will tell you, they don't have a job; they have one and a half jobs. Put on top of that the added task of *changing how they're operating* while still doing the role they were hired for. You're going to need buy-in from everybody. And the way to get there is by proving what's in it for everybody.

Implementing agile asks a ton of your employees and your organization. You'll be requiring your software engineers, analysts, testers, and managers to train for new roles, learn new tools and tracking mechanisms, and become fluent in agile jargon (and whatever dialect your organization goes with: scrum, XP, kanban, etc.). On top of their already loaded-down work schedule and to-do list, they're basically undergoing a new job training regimen.

> **We should be valuing individuals and interactions over processes and tools.**

To repeat that core tenet in the agile manifesto, we should be valuing individuals and interactions over processes and tools. It's easy to forget the human element when you're trying to oversee a complex organizational change. But until the robots come to replace us all, the process is dictated by people with full professional and personal lives—and all the emotions, hopes, fears, and desires that come with that. Software engineering is a fast-paced arena, and it can be volatile, stressful, and demanding. Explaining what exactly agile is, how it's going to help the organization, and how it's going to benefit *them* is, frankly, the right thing to do because it's good for them, and it's also good for the company.

Transitioning to agile is not solely about internal branding, or hanging motivational posters up in cubicles. A smart, front-footed organization will make the effort to reach out to individual employees and discuss why the company is changing and how the change will make the employee's life much better.

Some of that is the first step: assuaging their fears. Look, change is scary, especially when the change is coming to a routine and philosophy that's been ingrained into how somebody has operated for years, or even decades. Once you have the organizational perspective of the why, you can communicate what this means to them and reduce the fear.

Because the human condition trains us to fear the unknown, there may emerge this totally understandable reaction: "Wait! How do I fit into the new approach?" All people may be seeing right off the bat is how it could adversely impact their jobs, and if that happens, chances are slim they'll give the transition the benefit of the doubt. If they assume the worst and feel they'll be working themselves out of a job, why would they perform?

The first thing leadership needs to do is proactively address that. Hear and acknowledge the concerns. Talk about the education to come, and how, through training, the company will be able to transition employees into new roles. They've been important to the organization, and they have a place in the new world of agile. For those who aren't a good fit, as we'll see in chapter 5, the need for a break will be recognized by all parties. For the others, there may be a steep learning curve, but transforming the scope of their position on the team will come with tangible benefits:

More ownership. With a prioritized product backlog and responsibility pushed downward, away from managers, team members won't need bosses telling them what to do next. There won't be any orders being doled out and followed. It'll be a prioritized product backlog (or to-do list) with a shared definition of *done*.

Shared data through agile metrics about the amount of work actually being accomplished, what's missing from the upfront plan, what stumbling blocks occur, what's unforeseen, what commitments aren't being honored—all of this aggressive transparency feeds the trust of the team. Team members will be involved in the decision-making process early on in the agile approach and, as a result, feel more integral to the process. This is true ownership and accountability.

More happiness. Is there anything more soul crushing in the product engineering sphere than helping create something just to see it thrown out? To have all that work tossed aside for reasons never fully communicated to the team member? Agile greatly reduces that level of wasted time and effort. Decisions don't happen in a vacuum, and software engineers will be involved from the beginning in planning. The autonomy of teams, the inclusion of employees, and request for their feedback will properly value them within the organization and lead to improved company morale.

More productivity. Happier employees are more productive employees. They perform better; they have better energy and health. This may seem counterintuitive to the command-and-control ideology that has been taught at business schools, but there's data correlating happiness and productivity beyond simple paychecks. One research project showed that happy workers are around 12 percent more productive than unhappy ones.[5] Other studies have shown that happiness can increase "productivity by 31%, and accuracy on tasks by 19%, as well as a myriad of health and quality of life improvements."[6] The positive effects of autonomy and responsibility

---

5   University of Warwick, "New Study Shows We Work Harder When We Are Happy," March 21, 2014, press release, accessed September 18, 2018, https://warwick.ac.uk/newsandevents/ pressreleases/new_study_shows/.

6   Shawn Achor, "The Happiness Dividend," *Harvard Business Review,* June 23, 2011, accessed

on happiness are also well-documented.[7]

More money. Okay, it's crass, but essential. Higher productivity through agile means a business bringing quality products with more predictability to market at a quicker pace, and this will be reflected in the company's success and the employees' bonuses.

In some cases it may be enough just to say, "You'll make more money," to get employees fired up. That's true, and a better paycheck always helps get people on board with organizational change. But after a certain point, the level of salary stops being a motivating factor. Accentuating the *value* of each team member, the increase in responsibility, and the reduction of waste—these will achieve buy-in to the transition. And they're all part of the principles of agile: self-organizing teams, motivated individuals, face-to-face conversation, and reflection.

Agile's better work culture, not typically a shining by-product of command-and-control ideology, comes with greater care for employees, responsibility sharing, and clarity of vision. With a correct and holistic implementation of agile, you can be sure that managers are working actively to remove obstacles from the team's ability to finish work, sharing the targets of the project with team members, and encouraging collaboration from day one.

Figuring out what you're solving for by implementing agile can help focus the entire organization around goalposts; it also helps with adjusting your exact methodology to suit your short-term and long-term needs. And then communicating exactly what that vision is to your team members will help them get on board and put in the

September 19, 2018, https://hbr.org/2011/06/the-happiness-dividend; Shawn Achor, author of *The Happiness Advantage,* also opines that "the single greatest advantage in the modern economy is a happy and engaged workforce."

7   Diane Hoskins, "Employees Perform Better When They Can Control Their Space," *Harvard Business Review,* January 16, 2014, accessed September 19, 2019, https://hbr.org/2014/01/employees-perform-better-when-they-can-control-their-space.

necessary time to understand and adapt to an agile framework.

This transparency and respect for *everyone* associated with the engineering workflow is a hallmark of agile itself. After all, the fact finding in the discovery process leans on the staff-level employees and helps flesh out what that vision is going to be. The feedback I receive from employees who entrust me in a safe space with their view from the floor fits into making the organization the best run with the best outcomes.

> **This transparency and respect for *everyone* associated with the engineering workflow is a hallmark of agile itself.**

Prizing face-to-face interactions and open communication are also attributes of agile. They form the basis of the approach. So it makes sense that before instilling these as company values, you use these tools in talking with team members about agile itself. Starting the transformation with this kind of healthy dialogue, taking the view from fifty thousand feet up, will establish the expectation level for the rest of the transition and the new world for the organization. At the end of the day, it's always about the people—as the next chapter will expand on.

Chapter 5

IT'S THE PEOPLE (AND THE ORGANIZATION)

There's something grimly ironic about the fact that the name for the new modular rooms in offices for private calls and internal meetings is *pods*. Pod is also the name for a grouping of dolphins, and each group is hypercommunicative and hypercooperative. Far from being insular and walled off, pods of dolphins are highly social collectives, with each member staying alert for predators, helping one another navigate the ocean, observing their surroundings, and caring for each other intimately. It's not unusual for pods to interchange members, a kind of cross-functional team approach. In locations where there's an abundance of food—or a devastating enemy such as a tiger shark—pods have been known to join together to create a superpod to undertake the project of eating or defending.

The success and scientific fascination with dolphins is wrapped up in their socialization and group interaction. Their self-awareness and enhanced communication skills keep them leaps and bounds (literally, often) ahead of other animals. They will also quickly attend to sick or injured members of their pod, so close is the social bond. They recognize the importance of each team member.

Here's the truth. Your company could have the best tools, the best systems, and the best processes in place for organizational success, but if the people aren't working out, it'll be nearly impossible to perform at an optimal level. No matter how you slice it, it's always—*always*—about the people.

No matter how you slice it, it's always—*always*—about the people.

By the end of my initial conversation with executives who bring me in to fix a failing agile transformation, I can pretty much guarantee that there's one thing they need to do, and *fast:* review the people. Thorough engagement with a cross section of the teams will enable you to locate the bottlenecks and prescribe specific process and organizational changes.

Assessing the people is essential to implementing or improving agile. Are they all aligned with the same goals? Are they putting the organization's needs first, and concentrating on the customer? There are very few roles in a company that require absolute, deep-domain expertise at the expense of all other things. Give me somebody who has the right personality for collaboration and a readiness to transform over a me-first expert any day of the week, and five times on Sunday.

It's a sentiment reflected in both the agile manifesto and the twelve principles of agile: the most powerful lever an organization has is its people. There's no better way to improve software delivery, speed, quality, and efficiency than by ensuring the right team is in place with the right skill sets, the right behavior, a clear definition of who fits what role, and the culture to support all of this. The best teams in an agile environment are disciplined and self-organizing. The team members respect one another but hold one another accountable; and all of them concentrate on the end goal of value delivery to the customer.

This is another reason that the initial dialogue during the discovery weeks is so important. Hearing from the people on the ground about what the end-to-end process looks like—what everyone's roles are, what can be changed about the company—reveals how the organization as a whole is operating. You'll be able to tell who fits into the current culture, who'll be able to slot into the new requirements during the agile transformation, and who may need to be reassigned.

Valuing the people who comprise the organization comes with a shift, however. It asks of leadership to let go and trust their teams, to clarify roles and responsibilities, and to create a supportive work environment.

Because agile shifts the responsibility to autonomous, self-organizing teams, and entrusts them to hold one another accountable, having the right people aligned with the same goals is paramount.

Trusting Teams to Be Autonomous

Because agile shifts the responsibility to autonomous, self-organizing teams, and entrusts them to hold one another accountable, having the right people aligned with the same goals is paramount. Systems and processes can be designed around a highly functioning group whose members share an identical philosophy. But just try doing that with a team that can't produce together effectively, don't trust one another, or are wary of the new transformation. It'll be an uphill battle.

And that's true for leadership as well. We've looked at ways heads of engineering and other VPs can consciously or subconsciously obstruct agile. But sometimes leaders simply find themselves in the wrong role, transferred to a level that doesn't match their skill set. This poor fit ends up negatively affecting the team and process, and wasting time.

And hey, it's often not any fault of these managers. Sometimes they're put in a position where they can't help but fail. They've been working for years in a management capacity and repeating the methodology that's been built into the organization by tradition and history. Unfortunately, that process doesn't sit well with agile, and frankly, it doesn't get the best results out of a team.

It's tough to move from a command-and-control management style to one of vision, inspiration, and servant-leadership, removing obstacles and listening to feedback. If leadership is focusing on the wrong things, that'll trickle down to team members. If they require certain status reporting or ask for old data points, that'll also hinder team progress. Possibly the biggest hindrance to good results—and it's often because of an existing culture—is the lack of accountability for team members.

While it may seem as if leaders are asked to do *less* in agile, it actually takes a lot. It takes the ability to hold everyone accountable to the same standards. It takes somebody who's able to listen and value input and figure out how best to simplify the process for her team. It takes somebody who is able to maneuver the right people into the right roles.

And there's (part of) the rub. Meritocracy is rarely instituted across the board in any organization. There are only so many areas you can stock with your superstars. Very often department heads have to make critical decisions on personnel, but focus and problem-solving stems from the top. A well-functioning team needs a servant-leader who is able to coax the best performance out of her team, analyze the right metrics, and hold everyone equally accountable. And, at least according to some data analyses, one of the biggest motivators and productivity boosters out there is autonomy.[8]

Giving the team more autonomy and trusting team members to make the right decisions requires a mind-set shift that many in management won't be comfortable with, but it's part of the agile process. Now, we're not talking about instituting a Tony Hsieh Zappos-style holocracy, but a more self-organizing set of teams' demands that management become more involved on a commitment and responsibility-sharing level. How can leaders inspire and create vision and get the most out of employees?

Well, we have to *let go*. We have to acknowledge that there are staff-level stars under us who know more about the product or process, and we have to empower them to take the reins. Tap into these employees' knowledge—in the same way the initial discovery sessions do—and allow it to help shape the process. We have to take the commitment to learning new metrics seriously and recognize the tremendous effort employees are putting in to adjust their mind-sets and keep doing their jobs.

Trying to manipulate agile to fit the top-down leadership style that flourished under waterfall just won't work. That hierarchy doesn't prize input, and it looks to control the team rather than let the team control itself. Simply put, a good leader learns when to let go.

---

8   As we'll get into in chapter 7, in which we look at autonomy, mastery, and purpose, courtesy of Dan Pink. Daniel Pink, "The Puzzle of Motivation," lecture, 2009, TEDGlobal, accessed October 11, 2018, https://www.ted.com/talks/dan_pink_on_motivation?language=en.

Clear Roles and Responsibilities

While leadership is delegating responsibility, the team needs to make sure all its members know their roles and responsibilities. One of the biggest reasons teams fail in the agile process is a lack of clarity on this. It's something that needs to be delineated early in the process to reduce confusion and conflict. We all want to know how we fit into the machine. It puts our mind at ease to quantify what we do and what we bring to the table. Being able to define these gets everybody on the same page.

If team members can't pin down their actual roles in an agile transformation, it may be a result of a rushed implementation, or short shrift given to their education about their new duties. Outlining everyone's roles and how each role fits into the overarching agile principles puts everything in context.

The reason this is important goes back to one of the major tenets of the lean philosophy: eliminating waste, overlooked tasks, or redundancies that emerge from role confusion ends up consuming time. For example, consider the migration of code from an engineering to a staging environment. Depending on which team you're on, the person accountable for this task may change from a sole software engineer to a separate dev ops organization to, maybe, a case-by-case basis. Does everyone know who's responsible for the promotion? I've seen major confusion on this item alone, and it can cause bad bottlenecks.

This speaks to the standard of communication a team needs. Getting the end-to-end, top-down process steps in place ensures that everyone is operating from the same playbook. Who's going to be migrating the code on any given team? Who's responsible for the acceptance criteria—the work requester or the PO? Or the entire software engineering team?

There are standard exercises leadership can initiate when defining roles and responsibilities. Mapping out the design and capabilities of the organization, and diagramming the activities associated with each role under leadership can give management ways of assessing how and where each team member fits.

You can also see if each team member fits. Crystallizing roles and duties are necessary for assembling the right team with the right skills, and this isn't particularly easy in the transition to agile. Take the role of the business analyst: Under the waterfall methodology, the analyst is an internal expert who comprehensively understands the industry involved and the systems used. He defines and confirms requirements, does problem analysis, and shepherds the project through to presentation for management. Now, in an agile approach, that role shifts to that of a PO. It becomes less about having all the answers and solving in a vacuum. A good PO isn't a self-proclaimed subject matter expert; she's curious about the customer or end user and discovers the answers through feedback.

Instead of compiling requirements with technical specifications, the upfront documents are more narrative based—they're stories from the customer's point of view. Just the language used in the early part of software engineering symbolizes the focus shift from waterfall to agile. For example, waterfall requirements may be written as "Table A to be inserted with Parameter B so that functionality is updated with Attribute C." An agile story personalizes it, often with a hypothetical customer in the template: As a [user], I need to [action] so that [beneficial reason]. For example, "As a bank teller, I need to query customers' accounts so that I can tell them what their balances are."

This change in requirement language may seem small, but it highlights a large shift in behavior. Analysts in waterfall may not be able to transform into POs; their personalities are different, and the skill sets are different. Some will be able to accept the process of transformation and pivot through training to assuming the new role. But for others, it may not be a good fit. Assembling the best people in the best capacities involves coaching to remodel employees' behaviors within agile, as well as bringing in new blood from external pools.

For every calcified business analyst who can't adapt, there may be a portfolio manager who happens to have a great disposition for servant-leadership. It may be an easy adjustment for her to move from ordering status reports to influencing and inspiring team members. A proper assessment of team members before their transition to agile typically yields four categories of people who have:

- the right fit for the new role, and can start immediately in the position;

- the right fit for the new role, but will need some training and coaching to get up to speed;

- not the right fit for the new role, but the right fit for the company; steps should be taken to see where their skill set would be better utilized;

- not the right fit for the company at large; steps should be taken to ease them out and help them find a better organizational fit.

This last category can be the most stressful for leadership but also requires immediate action. In the previous chapter, I mentioned that assuaging the fears of the team members is good for morale when beginning the transformation. But it's also necessary to be honest. There are some personality types that simply won't be a good fit for the agile approach and the team's progress. You'll know it after a fifteen-minute conversation, or maybe, after a week. And it won't be a surprise to them or anyone around them that they're not a fit. You may even be met with a "Yeah, what took you so long?"

However, there are often some overlooked all-stars working in the company. I called them champions earlier in the book, and they deserve your attention because they can be the keys to the entire process. They're the mid-level all-stars who put the team first, software engineers or senior contributors who earn the respect of their peers. These are the folks who've been doing great work for six or seven years. They're flexible enough to bring on new techniques and aren't afraid to change midstream.

These are the people to empower. Just as they can be champions of the agile transition, they can also get more space to grow within the organization. They've proven they have the DNA to be successful—they have the right personality to experiment and they're bold enough to fail. They're the ones who can be brought into the review sessions to give feedback before the product is released.

These stars aren't the know-it-alls; they're the ones who help others solve problems and generally want to improve things for the company as a whole. Other workers gravitate toward them. If entrusting the team with more autonomy is the first step toward servant-leadership from the top, it begins here.

A Supportive Work Environment

The people determine the success of the company. You can design the systems and processes around your employees. To get the best work out of them, however, you have to change the culture and environment and make it conducive to bold, collaborative work.

In November 2015, Google released the results of a multiyear study titled "Project Aristotle: Reflecting on the Most Important Ingredients That Go into Successful Teams."[9] The results of this study were surprising to some but predictable to anyone who's ever spent time in a heavily collaborative field. The five most important dynamics were psychological safety, dependability, structure and clarity, the significance of the work, and the impact of the work. According to Google's report, "far and away" the most important of those five criteria was the first one: psychological safety. In its findings, Google added,

> In a team with high psychological safety, teammates feel safe to take risks around their team members. They feel confident that no one on the team will embarrass or punish anyone else for admitting a mistake, asking a question, or offering a new idea. An organization which creates a culture that allows members to take risks and fail spectacularly, which created a safe environment without fear of reprisal, allows for its team to be the best it can be.[10]

How important is psychological safety in a company that prizes flexibility and … well, agility? Consider that "positive emotions like trust, curiosity, confidence, and inspiration broaden the mind. … We become more open-minded, resilient, motivated, and persistent when we feel safe. Humor increases, as does solution-finding and divergent thinking—the cognitive process underlying creativity."[11]

In a complex field that requires an empirical process for adapting and problem solving based on feedback, the ability to fail in a safe

---

9   Charles Duhigg, "What Google Learned from Its Quest to Build the Perfect Team," *New York Times Magazine,* February 25, 2016, https://www.nytimes.com/2016/02/28/magazine/what-google-learned-from-its-quest-to-build-the-perfect-team.html.

10   re:Work, "Guide: Understand Team Effectiveness," accessed September 27, 2018, https://rework.withgoogle.com/print/guides/5721312655835136/.

11   Laura Delizonna, "High-Performing Teams Need Psychological Safety: Here's How to Create It," *Harvard Business Review,* August 24, 2017, https://hbr.org/2017/08/high-performing-teams-need-psychological-safety-heres-how-to-create-it.

environment and have continuous support will bring out the best in all employees, and that motivation will be infectious.

While improving the work environment for employee happiness and productivity through a safe space is not necessarily a new idea, it has been embraced by the most successful tech- and data-driven companies in America. Engaged and inspired employees make for a powerful, productive force. This all stems from leadership facilitation, especially as work and life blend. In its coverage of "Project Aristotle," the *New York Times Magazine* observed, "The behaviors that create psychological safety … are part of the same unwritten rules we often turn to, as individuals, when we need to establish a bond. And those human bonds matter as much at work as anywhere else. In fact, they sometimes matter more."[12]

A favorable environment begins with aligning goals. It means making sure that the right people are in place with the right skill sets, and it means getting rid of the ones who can't adapt. It means championing and empowering the midlevel stars, and letting go. It means reaching back to the agile manifesto, and making sure that the customer is coming first in decision making, and that the product and software engineering teams are working together with the same delivery goals and the same definition of *done.*

The software engineering world is complex. It's fast-moving, it's unpredictable, and requirements change constantly. To adapt to this, the organization and environment need to change to address that relative lack of stability. You have hard decisions to make when restructuring teams, and hard traditions to break along the way. But it's all in service of the most powerful lever your organization has: its people.

---

12 Charles Duhigg, "What Google Learned from Its Quest to Build the Perfect Team," *New York Times Magazine,* February 25, 2016, https://www.nytimes.com/2016/02/28/magazine/what-google-learned-from-its-quest-to-build-the-perfect-team.html.

Chapter 6

WAS EVERYONE IN THE COMPANY ON BOARD, OR JUST SOFTWARE ENGINEERING?

With the ongoing evolution of how and where products are sold, a lot of businesses position themselves as technology companies. They're tech driven, and their apps, platforms, or algorithms are what drive their income. Automobile companies are pouring millions into R&D for autonomous vehicles; clothing companies are doing the same for smart watches and smart clothing. Businesses such as Uber and Blue Apron don't even think of themselves as being in the ride-sharing or food-delivery service; they're both tech companies. Goodness knows Amazon isn't a retailer; its most (and possibly only) profitable line is AWS, its cloud computing services.

In this fad of treating everything as if it were tech, it's easy for agile to get lost in this morass as well. "Oh," some say when an organization is prepping for a switch to agile, "that's just for software engineering teams."

> **Believing that agile only has ramifications for software engineering, and therefore only engineering should be involved, is wrong-headed as well as dangerous for a company's process.**

Let's resurrect this busted myth from chapter 2 because it's a mistake that not only internal executives can make in an effort to streamline a transition but also outside consultants because of the tendency to rush implementations. Agile doesn't just change the way software engineers and testers behave. It impacts everyone. Believing that agile only has ramifications for software engineering, and therefore only engineering should be involved, is wrong-headed as well as dangerous for a company's process.

We've already talked about how undergoing an agile transformation requires everyone's buy-in, but I want to double down on it here. This is a change in the software engineering process that will have an impact on every stakeholder in the organization, and it's necessary for the transformation to keep all of the departments in mind for overview, training, and feedback.

Treating agile as "just a software engineering thing" subjects the company to potential major roadblocks and delays. Consider the product backlog, the main driver for actionable items in scrum. If this is a software-engineering-only agile transformation, how can product be involved in a coherent way to provide the features and user stories?

And if the software engineering team is altering the way it requests work from the business, and no other team has been informed about the changes to the landscape, what are the consequences?

Sometimes the CTOs or other executives embed me with just the software engineers. "Okay," they say, "here are the software engineers. Now change the way we do business." Again, when we're scaling agile, we have to take the time to do everything right. And that involves bringing everyone up to speed, even if not every department is immediately and directly impacted.

Now, when we refer to "everyone," we include two levels of staff. The first is within operations and technology, which doesn't just mean software engineering. It also includes the other facets of technology, such as storage, data, infrastructure, dev ops, and even security. The personnel in all these departments need to know software engineering's processes—not just the engineers and not just the technical lead.

The second level of inclusion is every other stakeholder.

That especially means the product team. This team is most closely associated with the operations and technology group and needs to be in the planning sessions constantly. More than once have I had an executive on the product team come to me, simply fuming. Turns out the software engineering department has been undergoing this whole transition, and now that millions of dollars have been invested, this department is only now telling the product team members that they've got to change as well—a *year* after the fact.

More than any other groups, product and software engineering need to have shared goals, shared principles and metrics, and the same definition of *done*. In fact, to ensure as little conflict as possible in the process, I generally advise that the agile overhaul be led by *both* of these teams. You disregard product at your own risk—and in violation of agile tenets.

If you're practicing (or adopting) scrum, there are three roles you have to fill: scrum master, team member, and PO. Product is literally a part of this methodology.

Product leadership has to operate closely with software engineering to make sure that goals are aligned, data points are agreed upon, and concerns are managed. They also have to set the roadmap or the vision for the overall strategy, an even more important directive in agile because of the consistent feedback and evolution of the product.

In larger organizations, there are two separate parts of the product team, both of which are essential. Product management is the liaison between engineering and the customer-facing departments such as marketing and sales, outlining the vision and writing the epics or features.[13] Product owners, on the other hand, work with the PM to understand what she wants from an initiative (a project comprising a set of features). Product owners then translate the specific requirements within the features into user stories for the team, which begin the conversation on how to address certain features. To put it a bit more simply, product management is the *why*, the PO is the *what*, and the software engineers and other team members that make that all happen are the *how*.

Getting product onboard on day one will not only help them understand why the work is changing, but also how that shift will manifest in communicating the needs of the customer, getting status updates, and the process at large. The product team may have its own methodologies in identifying customer value. If the product team's strategy doesn't mesh up with what software engineering is concentrating on, you will have two departments working from two

---

13 I like to think of this organization as product *marketing* management. While small businesses and start-ups may roll PMs and POs into the same job out of necessity, a separate product management department is an absolute must in a large company that's working with the customer-focused approach of agile.

different playbooks.

Whether the product team is responsible for owning relationships within the organization, setting the ground rules for software engineers, or having the grand vision for the software in the first place, it makes sense for the product team to be driving the transformation. Get product team members in there from the beginning, and let them help take the reins.

So agile doesn't impact just software engineering. But it doesn't impact just operations and technology and product either. Think about all the other stakeholders in the organization that need to know how the business is changing.

We're talking about a matter of degrees. Not every group has to be involved on a day-to-day basis, but any agile transformation should give an overview to all stakeholders so they feel they're a part of it and have input with the teams that are the focal point of the change. Involvement from initiation will make them less fearful and will allow the organization to dispel the myths right off the bat. They'll be able to get a handle on the changes and raise any concerns they may have.

Sales and marketing are often the conduit between company and customer. Some organizations have a different team for that—customer success, perhaps. These customer-facing departments can be considered ongoing stakeholders, so they'll be involved with the process repeatedly. Since they are the ones interacting with the clients, they'll be receiving a constant flow of feedback, and as a result will be raising more concerns and requesting work more frequently as well, which they do through product management. Sales and marketing need to participate as part of the process up front and also be brought back throughout to continue to be the customer's voice in engineering and improvement.

A department such as HR has less interaction with the process but is still affected. As noted in chapter 3, this department needs to grasp the new jargon and the new approach so they can actually fit the right people in the right positions and understand what the new job families are. If HR is left out of an overview, they might still be looking to staff vacant roles in agile with a project manager or business analyst—positions that are substantially different and require different skill sets from a scrum master or PO. New employees also have to possess that agile mentality—flexibility, autonomy, and collaboration—to succeed in the organization. If HR doesn't understand the new approach to roles, they won't be recruiting the right people.

Once the HR people figure out the job requirements for each of these positions, they don't have to be at every meeting, but that initial discussion and onboarding are crucial to their ability to maneuver in the new agile world. Same with the people from finance. If you bring them in for that synopsis and overview and educate them on how the software engineering processes will be different in agile, they'll be able to let operations and technology know how to track work and progress differently to honor software capitalization under SEC rules.

And what about the legal folks? They may not seem to be stakeholders, but what about when they're supporting contracts with customers and internal vendors? More than likely, they will need to comprehend the new approach to product engineering to structure work. Just making sure an organization is, head to toe, aware of the change from the fifty-thousand-foot level will keep questions and conflict to a minimum.

The amount of inclusion depends on the stakeholder. But I cannot overemphasize the importance of giving the organization an overview. If you're changing the way a major part of your company—and perhaps a major percentage of your employees—thinks and operates, you will want to fill everyone in on that. At the bare minimum, offer all the stakeholders half a day's worth of orientation to explain what agile is, what it isn't, what the myths are, how the software engineering teams will shift, and what's going to stay the same. Conveying how it impacts each organization and individual is critical. In some cases, there is no impact, and in many cases it may be minimal, but even so, it's important to cover that to remove fear.

Additionally, aligning ongoing stakeholders with the same data is another step in improving communication. Let's go back to the analogy of *Moneyball* we discussed earlier.

At the turn of the millennium, the Oakland Athletics began disregarding some of the older statistics that the game had held so dear for nearly a century. Batting average, often the main number traditional fans think about in baseball, is a simple stat that displays how often a batter reaches base because a ball he hit landed safely in the field: the number of hits divided by number of at-bats. One problem with this metric is that some of it has to do with luck—say, poor defensive positioning. But the larger problem is that it doesn't account for other ways the batter can reach base. The number-one thing batters need to do is not make outs. To its detriment, batting average doesn't account for the numerous times batters reach base via a walk. Enter OBP, the stat the As started highlighting, which does account for walks.

Now, can you imagine if the As told their minor-league-player engineering staff to concentrate on OBP . . . but their scouts looking at amateur talent were still focusing on batting average? New players coming into the organization might be very good at batted ball contact but wouldn't know how to draw a walk, making the job of the player engineering guys more difficult.

Now what if the major-league coaches were, as were the scouts, focused on batting average and told the players to stop taking pitches and drawing walks? Then all the work the engineering guys did just went out the window!

It's no different—and perhaps more stark, and more repeatedly confounding—in software engineering. Getting input from all of the stakeholders helps identify other considerations, and gears solutions toward the company's and clients' needs.

Forgetting other stakeholders can sometimes result from large consulting companies arriving with capital-*A* Agile plans and focusing solely on the software engineering team and engineering managers. While there's pressure from up top to onboard the new approach and get software engineering to hit the ground running, resist the urge to rush. It's incumbent on any consultant, and on the organization's executives as well, to take time to include everyone in at least one step of planning—even customers, maybe not up front but certainly in an overview orientation. It's easy to forget about them when you start getting into the weeds of the transformation, but it's right there in the third line of the manifesto: "Collaboration with customer instead of contract negotiations." The customers should be foremost in the company's mind with initiatives, user stories, design, and engineering, but it's about creating the product *in conversation* with them, instead of as a contract, which insinuates that the customers have no input, and must accept the product as a service.

There are other reasons to include the customer in the conversation. You're overseeing this tremendous overhaul, but did you remember that you've got to integrate with other companies? If Netflix is upping its deployments from four launches a year to eight, that's a pretty drastic change on its end. While each specific Netflix watcher doesn't need to be apprised of different launches, content providers that use them as their streaming platform in a B-to-B-to-C relationship, do. After all, they have a responsibility to *their* customers. Altering how and when Netflix gives them deliverables can have an impact not only on the way they operate but also on their sense of stability and predictability.

Collaborate with your business customers. Let them in on the process of the changes, and see how you can extract value from them. Tell them how much their feedback will become integral to the improvement of the product, and how they won't have to wait for total overhauls but, instead, be privy to iterative upgrades.

Customers can be just as hard a sell when it comes to changes, especially if it affects how and when they receive the product and what the changes in functionality will be. Communicating with them on how the new engineering approach will alter their relationship with the product is key to reducing unease and keeping loyalty.

Agile may have been spawned from the minds of software engineers, but it is by no means just about software engineering, nor is it just for software engineering. The specifics of how agile works and changes priorities are points that every department in an organization needs to know. It's necessary for employees to understand how other teams are operating, and how their own is expected to. But agile's approach to workflow accentuates general principles about self-organization, focusing on customers, and ensuring good, productive communication, values that every department in an organization would agree to.

Or at least, they should. And in a company with a conducive culture, they will.

Chapter 7

LET CULTURE BE THE PATH

So what are we talking about when we talk about culture? With all the phrases out there about it—"Culture is king" and "Culture eats strategy for breakfast," to name just two—it's easy to see how the idea can get away from the meaning.

Let me propose this definition: Culture is the result of your set of values working in the operation of your business. Or, as my friend John Ballay says, in excellent metaphorical terms, if your company's goals and vision for the organization are your coordinates, your culture is the path you take to get there.

It's your values that make it clear what you protect in your organization. Turning those values that comprise the company into the guideposts and landing point can only happen when the culture is adopted and adhered to by everyone in the organization.

That said, the organizational behavior theorist and cocreator of LeSS (large-scale scrum), Craig Larman,

If your company's goals and vision for the organization are your coordinates, your culture is the path you take to get there.

says that "culture follows structure," to explain that only when the underlying system shifts can the culture and people's behavior change.[14] Here's the thing: both are right. Every company is different, and some large, staid organizations may have to make fundamental changes to allow for the culture to take hold. But at the end of the day, we're arguing semantics. A conducive culture is necessary for businesses to progress past inertia, and focusing solely on processes or structures misses this.

The honest truth is that if there isn't a culture in place to achieve a sense of adaptability and change, and fertile ground for innovative thinking, those processes and structures won't succeed by themselves. It's like constructing a brand-new condo on top of a pie crust. Forget selling the units; you won't even get the building to stay upright because the foundation is so flaky and unstable from the start. But at many companies, unlike the pie crust, it's not because the foundation is so brittle but because it's so steel-reinforced and intransigent that it doesn't allow for change.

Given the amount of ink (digital and otherwise) spilled on the

---

14   Craig Larman, "Larman's Laws of Organizational Behavior," accessed December 28, 2018, https://www.craiglarman.com/wiki/index.php?title=Larman%27s_Laws_of_Organizational_Behavior .

concept of culture leading the way, it's become an accepted fact that a company needs to have a culture conducive to evolution if its strategy for winning in the marketplace is going to work.

But as we've all seen, that's far easier said than done.

It's a fairly normal occurrence when I'm working with a new institution that somebody approaches me and says "Okay, Jason, you're here to implement something big and give us a transformational change. That sounds great. It's never gonna happen."

It's true: Other consultants and big-vision experts have tried to enact systemic change within organizations and crashed and burned magnificently. There are a lot of nods of approval when the big picture of transformation is displayed at the outset, but what happens when it comes time to actually take the steps? Those nods turn to frowns.

It's easy to give lip service to a holistic change. Walking the walk, however—that's something else. And that's why it's important to commit and have management lead the way.

And that all stems from the top down. It's easy to give lip service to a holistic change. Walking the walk, however—that's something else. And that's why it's important to commit and have management lead the way.

What does an effective company with a winning culture look like? Well, here's some data. In a March 2018 report, McKinsey stated that "[b]ased on our research of over 1,000 organizations that encompass more than three million individuals, those with top quartile cultures … post a return to shareholders *60 percent higher* than median companies and *200 percent higher* than those in the bottom quartile" (emphasis added).[15]

Those are big numbers. And at this point, I don't think anyone would necessarily argue that culture isn't important. But it's also crucial to enabling an agile transformation in an organization.

According to McKinsey, an incredibly small number of companies are actually able to achieve an organization-wide transformation: "The No. 1 problem they cite is culture."[16] The annual *State of Agile* report repeatedly points to three major areas that employees cite as obstacles to agile adoption and scaling: organizational culture at odds with core agile values, general organizational resistance to change, and poor management support.[17]

So, let's take a look at your practices. What's going on there? What are the values your company currently supports? Let's define them. The values of a company show up in their actions: what they protect and what they hold dear.

Attempting an organizational transformation can hit some entrenched obstacles pretty quickly, and when it does, it becomes clear that what the company truly values is the tradition and regimented practices they're accustomed to. Maybe it's the bottom line or the revenue stream. Asking a company to let revenue be of a lower priority during the change to a new process won't be easy for managers who feel beholden to preserving it.

So, the first couple of steps in an agile transformation tend to go okay: There are movements toward collaboration and face-to-face communication. Helpful feedback is coming in and the prioritized

---

15   Carolyn Dewar, "Culture: 4 keys to why it matters," McKinsey & Company, March 27, 2018, accessed October 10, 2018, https://www.mckinsey.com/business-functions/organization/our-insights/the-organization-blog/culture-4-keys-to-why-it-matters.

16   Aaron De Smet, "Culture Can Make or Break Agility," McKinsey & Company, February 26, 2018, accessed October 10, 2018, https://www.mckinsey.com/business-functions/organization/our-insights/the-organization-blog/culture-can-make-or-break-agility?cid=other-eml-alt-mip-mck-oth-1803.

17   VersionOne, *12th Annual State of Agile Report*, April 9, 2018, accessed October 11, 2018, https://explore.versionone.com/state-of-agile/versionone-12th-annual-state-of-agile-report.

backlog is working out well. But all of a sudden, managers start to get nervous about the revenue stream. Then, levels of control start getting in the way. Managers request detailed specificity in upfront documentation. Funding for a project gets tied up in tiers of approval. Decisions become escalated again. The company that was so gung-ho on undergoing the transformation is all of a sudden showing risk aversion because too much is on the line. And the transformation? Well, as they said, "It's never gonna happen."

I get it. Change is hard. Stakeholders want answers. You're on the hook.

There are a lot of fundamental changes to its mind-set a company needs to undergo to make the culture conducive to change. Let's bring back the idea that executives need to "let it go." That's right: it's not just an anthem for Princess Elsa in *Frozen* anymore. Leadership needs to let go.

Leadership needs to let go.

Our values and behaviors reflect what we want to protect in the organization. And what if your company is repeatedly putting the revenue stream and traditional policies and thinking ahead of your employees and your customers? Well, then it's clear that the priorities aren't in the agile frame of mind. Your culture has to be about your people, and your actions have to portray that.

That command-and-control, top-down hierarchy? It has to change. The company has to be able to delegate responsibility and trust self-organizing teams to bring their full knowledge to making the right decisions, and take ownership of the projects. Cross-functional teams have to be allowed to blossom, breaking up siloed departments. Management has to do a lot less managing and a lot more leading, supporting, coaching, envisioning, and inspiring. Servant-leadership must be internalized and committed to.

You have to be able to stomach failure. Even more than that, you have to be able to *celebrate* failure. My friend and fellow agile coach extraordinaire John Krewson likens failure to all the prior drafts of any great work of literature. How many drafts of a masterpiece book were written? Fifty? Seventy-five? How many went to print? One.

Software engineers are part of the same process. We shouldn't expect the code they write to be perfect from the first prototype any more than we should expect J. K. Rowling to write the perfect version of *Harry Potter* on her first draft. Getting things wrong and receiving constructive feedback is extraordinarily valuable; it's how we make things better and suit our customers more. Averting risk and playing it safe and tepid won't put your company in a better position to succeed, it'll make it irrelevant. As Pixar's cofounder Ed Catmull said, "Failure is a manifestation of learning and exploration. If you aren't experiencing failure, then you are making a far worse mistake: you are being driven by the desire to avoid it. And, for leaders especially, this strategy—trying to avoid failure by outthinking it—dooms you to fail."[18]

You may already consider yourself a customer-centric company, but the steps you take in putting your people first and living up to the challenges of the agile culture will help shift you even further toward that model. Organizations that do this see the payoff in terms of better quality, more predictability, and quicker delivery of viable products.

Make it about the people, so the culture can take hold with each and every employee. That way, the agile transformation and projects can succeed and the customer can truly come first.

How can you create a culture in which the employees feel properly valued and an integral part of the organization? How can they be rewarded in a way that fosters their personal commitment to the company? Money, right?

---

18   Ed Catmull, with Amy Wallace, *Creativity, Inc.*, New York: Random House, 2014, p. 109.

Nope.

Remember back in chapter 4 when I said that after a certain point, the level of salary stops being a motivating factor? It's true, and there's data to back that up. As two noted behavioral economists observed, "Emotional well-being levels increase with salary levels up to a salary of $75,000—but that they plateau afterwards."[19] Basically, after you reach a certain salary, money isn't a motivating factor anymore.

In fact, according to some research, extrinsic motivators such as money can actually end up having a *negative* effect on performance.[20] So, how does a company reward people within the organization for a job well done besides salary and bonus? Make them heard, make them appreciated, and make them essential. There are numerous ways a company can show its team members how valuable they are that move beyond extrinsic motivators. And once applied, it'll seep into the culture of the organization.

Give the teams and employees autonomy. Empower them, so they take ownership of their projects and feel they're more than just cogs in a machine, that their decisions carry weight. It's scary, sure, getting rid of those levels of approval and management. But let's return to Catmull: "The antidote to fear is trust. Trusting others doesn't mean that they won't make mistakes. It means that if they do (or if you do), you trust they will act to help solve it."[21]

I once worked at a company that had strict protocol and admin rights to its machines. This is common: it helps protect against phishing attacks and other security concerns. But one of the software

---

19   Tomas Chamorro-Premuzic, "Does Money Really Affect Motivation?" *Harvard Business Review*, April 10, 2013, accessed October 12, 2018, https://hbr.org/2013/04/does-money-really-affect-motiv.

20   Daniel Pink, "The Puzzle of Motivation," lecture, 2009, TEDGlobal, accessed October 11, 2018, https://www.ted.com/talks/dan_pink_on_motivation?language=en.

21   Ed Catmull, with Amy Wallace, *Creativity, Inc.,* New York: Random House, 2014, p. 124.

engineers in a small group had a great idea that would shave a ton of time off installations. The problem was it required getting him and his team admin access to their own laptops. It was denied. Now, I'm not saying whether that was right or not. The disheartening part was that his suggestion *wasn't even entertained*. Management acknowledged it was a good idea but didn't have the time to devote to exploring it and didn't think it would pass muster with security. This great idea never reached the next level.

Do you think that software engineer has been motivated since then to do any creative, innovative thinking?

Compare that anecdote to what the Australian software company Atlassian began doing in 2005. Every quarter, engineers have twenty-four hours to work on anything they want. It could be related to their operations, or it could just be some quirk they've been mulling over in their minds. And during this exciting interval, employees create inspiring things that they then show and tell to their coworkers: hacks, prototypes, code patches that never would have come to fruition without the company saying, "Sure! Go for it!"

Atlassian is not the only company that asks its employees to break out of the mold of static thinking within their jobs. Google famously encourages its workers to devote 20 percent of their office time to side projects. Most notably, this has led to the creation of Gmail (as well as Google Maps, Google News, and so forth).[22]

As a report in *Harvard Business Review* revealed, "The power of choice and autonomy drives not only employee happiness but also motivation and performance."[23] When teams and employees are entrusted with decision making and given the power to innovate

---

22   Daniel Pink, "The Puzzle of Motivation," lecture, 2009, TEDGlobal, accessed October 11, 2018, https://www.ted.com/talks/dan_pink_on_motivation?language=en.

23   Diane Hoskins, "Employees Perform Better When They Can Control Their Space." *Harvard Business Review,* January 16, 2014, accessed October 12, 2018, https://hbr.org/2014/01/employees-perform-better-when-they-can-control-their-space.

with positive recognition from leadership, the company can end up with a happier and more productive group of workers.

Autonomy and delegation of decision making are not the only intrinsic motivators. Daniel Pink's book *Drive* lists autonomy as the first of three such stimuli. Mastery, the desire to improve ourselves at a skill or in a field that's important to us, is the second. How can a company support this? Here are some possibilities: Allow employees to find opportunities for growth within the organization; help them find training, or education, that develops that skill set, even paying for it as a means of investment; or create mentor programs within the company that allow on-the-job advice and counseling.

The third of Pink's intrinsic motivators is purpose, the feeling that what we do creates something bigger and more meaningful than ourselves. When leadership is able to create a vision and a set of goals that the entire company can rally behind and align itself with, that helps institute the culture that builds the path to get there.

All three of these concepts help make employees feel they're more—rightfully more—than just employees. They're self-organizing, innovative thinkers, improving their own craft in the service of a larger idea with actual impact. This is the kind of motivation that will get your team members energized, productive, and committed.

And remember this all stems from the top down. Culture doesn't just happen; it starts from the top and becomes part of the organization. So, leadership has to take the helm in instituting it and reflecting the values of the company. When it learns to let go of managing and delegate instead, this empowers and inspires the other things we've discussed: engaging stakeholders, promoting transparency and communication, and holding people equally accountable.

We know how demoralizing it can be when people face different standards. All team members must be held accountable to meet the same set of values that the organization has set out. If there are people in the chain who aren't working out, who can't meet the goals that the team has prescribed, or aren't being collaborative, don't reassign them, don't overlook it, and for goodness' sake, don't reward it.

Real meritocracies are few and far between in the business world, but the deleterious impact that lack of accountability can have on other employees is substantial. As I said, if given the choice between an intelligent expert who cordons herself off from the rest of the group and follows her own set of guidelines, as distinct from a team player who's up to problem-solve, give me that collaborator every single time.

Changing requirements, accepting feedback, reflecting, and adapting are core principles within agile. Experts who do best by themselves work well with some organizations but not in the collaborative, communicative teams of agile. Consider a November 2015 study out of Loyola University of Chicago that found that "those who perceive themselves as experts tend to exhibit more closed-minded behavior."[24]

As Reed Hastings, CEO of Netflix, has said, you should get rid of these "brilliant jerks." "Some companies tolerate them. For us, the cost to effective teamwork is too high."[25] The brilliant jerk doesn't have a place in the agile company. His main focus is himself and his methodology. No matter how valuable the person's mind and technique, if he can't adapt to the agile approach and the company's vision, it won't be a good fit. The probability that he'll accept other viewpoints or adapt to a product's evolving needs isn't worth the gamble.

---

24 Olivia Goldhill, "Science Says Those Who Think They Are Experts Are More Likely to Be Closed-Minded," *Quartz,* November 1, 2015, accessed October 12, 2018, https://qz.com/538308/science-says-those-who-think-they-are-experts-are-more-likely-to-be-closed-minded/.

25 Jim Schleckser, "Why Netflix Doesn't Tolerate Brilliant Jerks," *Inc.,* February 2, 2016, accessed October 11, 2018, https://www.inc.com/jim-schleckser/why-netflix-doesn-t-tolerate-brilliant-jerks.html.

All of which leads to this: Leadership has to be able to get rid of that brilliant jerk. You have to be able to make the tough decisions with personnel, just as you have to make the tough decisions to alter what your sense of a manager is and how delegation happens. It's difficult to get rid of somebody with obvious talent.

But it's these tough decisions that show executive commitment to the agile transformation and to what an agile culture looks like. It doesn't take much leadership to make the easy decisions, such as firing someone who routinely misses deadlines. But replacing a senior sales person who's responsible for a ton of your revenue? That's very hard—even if he or she is a jerk. And that's the kind of accountability that's important to honoring your vision and goals. That's true leadership in this realm.

Another significant aspect of leadership, just like finding the value in failure, is finding value in *not knowing*. In an agile world, where we're relying on the customer for feedback toward improvement, saying "I don't know" has its own rewards. But there has to be a conducive culture and open psychological space to allow us to admit that we don't know. Because that's not often how we're recognized and compensated. It's especially hard for a leader to say, "You know what? Beats me. Let's find out."

Think about how tough it is, as a parent, to tell your kid you don't know why the sky is blue or how the television works. We often find ourselves making something up so we can retain that kind of power and respect—because parents (and leaders) are supposed to have the answer. But there's real strength and long-term value in telling your child that although you don't know, you can look it up together. This empowers your kid to take ownership over finding the solution.

It's the same thing with your team. Acknowledging you don't

have all the answers, and being receptive to feedback and input, creates real transparency and collaboration. It takes away the hierarchical barriers that can obstruct teams from doing their best problem solving, and it honors your commitment to the values of an open, agile company.

Your culture is the path toward your vision and your goals. It's not just the amenities in your office, motivational posters with images of kittens hanging off tree branches, or giving people cake on their birthdays. And it's not even just the values but, instead, the total personality you and everyone in the organization take on, which informs your decisions and actions. Your goals are your end point, and your culture leads you to it. Accepting risk and failure, being truly open to change, and honoring accountability all help build the route there.

Let your people be the focal point of that path. Make your culture about your people by empowering them, respecting them, motivating them, and giving them room to grow and learn, and achieving your vision will be closer than you can imagine.

Chapter 8

DO WE KNOW WHERE WE ARE TODAY?

One of the key components of a consistent culture is ironing out the kinks, the aberrations in a company's personnel, encompassing the people, the roles, and the actions. I mentioned rewarding those mid-level all-stars and excising the "me-first" experts who weren't going to fit in with the agile approach. If the results of culture can be seen in the values and actions of all your team members, you're going to need to make sure everyone is working from the same playbook, both in approach and strategy. Part of bringing everyone together under an agile framework, and making sure they're all solving for X, is ensuring that the different teams—even when they're not colocated—are looking at the same metrics, tracking work with the same platforms, and following the same reporting processes. Because it's very possible that a poor agile implementation has left employees operating various tracking systems, barely entering data, not even knowing *which* data they're entering (or which is important), and—for a company that's suddenly supposed to be cross-functional—in the dark about other teams' progress. So, forget about them "knowing themselves"; they don't even know what tracking tool to open up.

After leadership takes the helm in assuring that the values and principles of the organizational culture are the same for all team members, and that everyone's buying into the agile approach and what that entails, it's incumbent on management to make sure that the strategies for tracking are adhered to by all relevant departments.

What's Your Baseline?

Let's go back to understand the baseline of where you are today, and what you're trying to solve for by transitioning to agile. If you say that you want your software engineering process to be more predictable, or produce software with fewer defects, that's great, but what are you measuring that against right now? Does everyone across your departments know it? Do all your employees even know it's a problem? That's a key ingredient in true transparency: being able to convey your company's position to everybody involved. If you don't know the baseline from where you're starting the transformation, it'll be hard to measure the success. How are you going to make sure all the disruption and overhaul was worth it without something to compare it to?

None of the data accumulation will amount to a hill of beans if you don't know where you are right now—if you don't know yourself. Let's say that through your applied methodology, you want to improve the speed of your deployments, specifically with lead time, the period from request to delivery. Well, a lot of steps happen in there. There's the creation of initiatives, features, and user stories; product puts together a prioritized backlog and works with software engineering to reorder and commit to the top needs; then development gets underway. Finally, there's the deployment. Lead time is a very important way of measuring productivity. If leaders come to me and declare they want their team to improve speed *but can't tell me what their existing lead time is*, that's a problem. If your company spends the capital, in terms of money, labor, and humans, in implementing agile, you better be able to point to quantitative improvements based on tracking data, starting from where you are right now.

Standardizing the Tracking Tool

Whenever we talk about communication and the need for face-to-face interaction, my friend John Krewson refers to what he calls the "bus rule." Basically, if people aren't located within the length of a bus from one another, they'll use the phone. Buses, typically, are about forty feet long. So what John theorizes—and I'd bet he's dead-on—is that if coworkers are more than about forty feet away from one another, instead of taking the seven seconds to have physical contact with somebody, they'd rather pick up the phone and call. That's how much we avoid looking somebody in the eye. If normal interaction is met with that kind of resistance, think about what it's like making sure people are communicating on essentials in workflow.

Getting your team members out of their vacuum chambers can start with standardizing the tracking tool they're using. I've often seen companies try to implement a certain tool—VersionOne, Jira, RallyCA, Pivotal Tracker—but software engineering teams end up only using it on a superficial level, entering the very bare minimum of information to honor finance rules on software capitalization. Meanwhile, on the platform they've always been using and are comfortable with, they continue to provide the real details and the comprehensive project plan. And then once a week, a project manager has to go into the standardized tracking tool and enter all of those real details herself. It's redundant and wasteful. Each team member should be providing the details in the same tracking tool, giving leadership timely and accurate info, and keeping the project managers from repetitive work.

Metrics and KPIs

The first step in consistent work tracking is identifying which key metrics your business cares about. Which data points can the team use as a diagnostic tool to course-correct? Which key performance indicators can leadership use to track progress? Once you know which measurements are important, you can define those norms, train your teams in how to use the tracking tool comprehensively, and ensure that everyone's operating on the same cadenced iterations. Finally, make sure everyone's looking at the same ingredients and entering data accurately—on whatever parameters your organization wants to measure speed, quality, or predictability. Using the same tool and knowing your organization is working on certain constancies (say, improving lead time) only helps insofar as you're looking at the same metrics.

No matter which methodology your team uses within the agile approach, KPIs are the guideposts for the process and measuring progress while also ensuring that the process is in cohesion with the organization's strategy and values. They help teams analyze what's working and what isn't, how to plan for following iterations, and whether the strategic goals are being successfully pursued.

Which KPIs your teams are tracking are, ultimately, tied to what goals you have and what methodology you apply to achieve them.[26]

---

26   This may go without saying, but just in case there's ambiguity: KPIs are not the same as

There may be XP-associated metrics that track code review and customer engagement, or kanban-associated metrics such as cumulative flow, or any number of others for scrum, LeSS, or crystal.

As referred to earlier, lead time is one of a host of metrics that your team could pursue, depending on your objectives. There are other data sets that you'll want clarity on such as cycle time. Cycle time is a component of lead time, measuring the period between a task being taken up by the software engineering team and its readiness for deployment. There's also predictability. Your software engineer team wants to deliver sixty features in a certain time period? Great, what's your end result? Were all sixty delivered, or was it fifty? And throughput: How many work items are done in a given period of time?

But remember that teams have to be on the same page as to what those specific metrics even are. You're tracking quality by measuring the number of defects per iteration? Great, but does the team know how to categorize defects? Are they severe, as in an all-hands-on-deck defect when the system shuts down? Where are the defects found? During engineering or after the release to the customer? Is there an upward trend with the defects? Know the indicators you're looking for and make sure team members are all tracking the same ones.

These are some of the simple metrics that agile practitioners may use to improve workflow. Different methodologies will also focus on different things, as will the scope of your company's improvements. But knowing what those improvements are geared to solving, and which metrics are worth following to get a picture of your orga-

---

metrics. The values that are aligned with your overall business goals or objectives are themselves "key," and those can be your KPIs; the values measured that *support* those KPIs in activities are themselves the metrics. Another way to say it: KPIs track whether you achieve the goals, and metrics track the process of reaching them.

nization's progress, is necessary to a successful transformation and aligning everyone's work.

While autonomy and delegation are absolute musts in the agile approach, applying standards across all teams is one thing managers should absolutely be doing as part of their larger envisioning and inspiring protocol. So, prescribe for all the disparate teams when iterations will start, what the time box is, and which metrics will be studied, based on all team members using that same time box. And then *train them to track and log them*. Part of that agile empowerment is entrusting the team members to be responsible for updating the data themselves, instead of using the old method: waiting until two o'clock in the afternoon on a Friday for the PMs to go into the tool and complete updating the status themselves.

While governance isn't a term that anyone in agile wants to throw around, leadership still has to take monitoring into consideration when normalizing standards. Call it "data hygiene," making sure everything is clean, healthy, and operating smoothly.

Tracking work and aggregating KPI data for observation and decision making can be time-consuming, but it's part of an overall strategy that is extremely effective—at least when done accurately and comprehensively. Bringing back the stat-heavy baseball team as an example, if the various departments of base running, hitting, and fielding were all entering bare minimum information on their players' development, the aggregate picture certainly wouldn't be the full representation of a player's productivity or progress. Frankly, you can imagine how wasteful having all that data would be in such a scenario.

Centralized tracking tools that companies push their teams toward can be particularly helpful, modified for keen transparency between departments. But it only works if thorough attention is given with real-time information. Often, and especially with businesses sporting offices in different states and countries, team members fill out only the skeletal essentials, rendering the tool utterly useless. Gleaning the whole story from the data requires wholesale buy-in. Making sure your team members are entering the work at regular time intervals and not cutting corners is time intensive but worthwhile.

We're asking for all of this workflow tracking and metric retrieving for comparison and refinement to find out where drag or bottlenecks are and how we can keep improving. Agile companies are always in a stage of retrospection and analysis, figuring out how to better the process. You can monitor statuses and learn a lot more from the numbers to figure out how you're doing, or where you can improve. It's another level of transparency that allows the business to understand the progress.

Once you figure out what the KPIs are, what your current baseline is, and what your work items are for each iteration, leadership needs to monitor that the tracking is actually happening in the first place. And once it does, managers become an integral part of this; they also have to look at and analyze that data. This is another place where leadership is on the hook. If we've gone through the trouble to train all these employees to make sure they're entering the specific data and reporting on the right metrics we're asking them to, management better be looking at the reports that we're actually tracking. These metrics are presented to executives to make sure that resources are properly being allocated to goals that are consistent with the strategy. If leadership isn't using the data—or even *looking* at it—then it's reporting for the sake of reporting, and that's tremendously disheartening for the team members whose time and work you should be respecting.

Face Time, not FaceTime

My friend's bus rule also speaks to the difficulty of communication in an increasingly technology-dependent world, where people can take the option of hiding behind screens all day. But one of the most important agile principles states that "the most efficient and effective method of conveying information to and within an engineering team is face-to-face conversation." This is where you're able to drive efficiency and improve productivity. Get out from behind emails and PowerPoint presentations, and have that face-to-face with team members. It's another step toward showing employees how valued they are, leading to strong, loyal, and trustworthy teamwork.

> **Get out from behind emails and PowerPoint presentations, and have that face-to-face with team members. It's another step toward showing employees how valued they are, leading to strong, loyal, and trustworthy teamwork.**

Think about our dolphin friends again. While they do well with echolocation and body language to convey a lot of information such as "food's over here," or "hey, pretty sure there's a shark up ahead," much of their interaction and communication is actually physical. They gently bump and touch each other to emit friendliness … and ratchet that up to aggressive bumping to emit competitive vibes. That's a kind of communication and interaction they can't enjoy from clicks and whistles a quarter mile away.

For humans, a lot of communication is nonverbal as well. We read a lot from one another's gesticulations, head and eye movements, and other sorts of body language. We may not slap our flippers in the water to signify hunger, but it's easy enough to gauge whether a point in a meeting lands on somebody just by looking at her. Will a PO know with certainty that the rest of her scrum team understands what the requirements (through select user stories) are if she's not located with the team in person, watching their mannerisms?

When it comes to the kind of reliance on actual face time (not video conferences) I'm advocating, smaller organizations have an easier go of it. With fewer resources and a smaller footprint, chances are that the PO and PM are the same person. In a start-up, that person could be sitting fifteen feet away from sales *and* software engineers. There's no need to break the jobs into two roles. Larger companies, however, may see communication and interaction problems out the wazoo as they deal with a broad swath of employees living in far-flung cities or countries, speaking different languages (both verbal and programming), and being comfortable with only certain methods.

So, here's something incendiary: I believe that if you choose distributed teams offshoring, you're choosing against agile.

If part of your team is in San Francisco, another part's in Dallas, and a third part is in New York City, you're never going to enjoy the efficiency and productivity benefits of full team face-to-face interaction.

Same thing with offshoring, which makes distributed teams even more pronounced, with software engineering and QA in India, but product management and business in the USA. From a command-and-control spreadsheet perspective, offshoring makes sense. You've got a software engineer in your office's flagship city who costs just under $200,000 a year, while one in India charges an hourly fee of $75. The latter is appealing from the direct cost side. But I would argue that it's actually cheaper overall to pay for the in-house talent who's colocated with the rest of the team than for the overseas software engineer.

Think about the hidden expenses. A time difference can slow a process down by days. Let's say you send an email to a designer in Bangalore at 9 a.m. EST on a Tuesday. He doesn't receive it until twelve hours later, and you don't receive *his* response until 9 a.m. EST on Wednesday. That's a full day lost, to say nothing of any follow-up questions and clarifications, which are usually standard. Phone calls or video conferences will run into challenges of time as well. A conversation about the process may take place at 6 a.m., one software engineer's time, and 6 p.m., another's time. That kind of onus on employees' schedules does not have the people's interests at heart or ensure the best work, and it violates a few agile principles, to boot.

Agile values real-time communication and relies on trust and transparent collaboration to build the teamwork, not to mention the need for interaction between certain stakeholders and the software engineering team. Any kind of roadblocks to these ingredients can be pretty darn detrimental to that end goal of quality and iterative product releases.

When you add up these hidden costs, in time lost through waiting and abused through bad scheduling, and the overall cost of less-than-perfect communication, it may indeed be a better option for a company to colocate.

But in truth, many companies just can't feasibly be living as start-ups do. Yes, increased volume leads to increased complexity, but for international companies with a large footprint, you have to make it work. Ultimately, you need your team members in the same place, if not geographically due to the reality of the business, then certainly mentally, as it pertains to what and how you're tracking, how the processes are pursuing the ultimate organizational goals, and in the overall values and actions of each employee.

While the reasons for transitioning to agile may be similar between companies, each business is its own unique model. The tracking system and metrics you choose to follow for the greatest efficiency, predictability, and quality will be tailored for your organization. How your business acts and reacts will be different from others, even though they may have similar issues to yours. Everything about *your* company, your culture, your values, and your personnel is different, as is how you accumulate the metrics and the tracking data.

Because, at the end of the day, we're all unique, and that applies to businesses as well as humans. And you can't just copy and paste what your competitor is doing … as we'll find out in the next chapter.

Chapter 9

DON'T COPY AND PASTE ANOTHER COMPANY'S SUCCESS

In 2011, Spotify was at a crossroads: The Swedish company was growing quickly and needed to add more bodies to its engineering team, but it still valued its start-up persona and ability to stay flexible. Over the next few years, Spotify continued to blossom, increasing its workforce from 100 to 3,500, IPOing with a $20 billion valuation. It's now a company with a substantial international footprint, and yet, somehow, it has remained nimble, using what it calls "Agile à la Spotify," a brief but complete appendix that expresses its agile values and culture, and guides how it works.[27]

---

27   Joakim Sundén, "Agile à la Spotify," Spotify Labs, March 20, 2013, accessed October 26, 2018, https://labs.spotify.com/2013/03/20/agile-a-la-spotify/.

This appendix highlighted five aspects of agile that were particularly important at Spotify (continuous improvement, iterative engineering, simplicity, trust, and servant leadership), and identified how employees at the company would help work to uphold those guideposts. It became a manifesto of sorts, and was hung up on walls in the offices as a reminder.

Spotify discovered a methodology that fit who it was and what it was trying to accomplish. Popularized in a widely read white paper by Henrik Kniberg and Anders Ivarsson,[28] the Spotify team instituted new groupings of team members called tribes, squads, chapters, and guilds. It accentuated autonomy, direct contact with stakeholders, observing and removing obstacles, daily sync meetings, face-to-face communication—all the hallmarks of agile and scrum but tailored to fit exactly where the business was. It has been adapted over the years to accommodate company growth.

Spotify created this customized approach through introspection and analysis, and numerous attempts—and failures—at scaling agile in a way that would work for its teams. Of course, with the rumors of Spotify's success and the publication of the white paper came numerous imitators. Companies looking for a shortcut to their own scalable agile transformation thought that just replicating what the music streaming company did would suit them well. But Spotify had a particular situation when it had self-organizing squads picking their own projects. Spotify was growing exponentially, was hugely successful and European, and had a culture of trust and independence already baked into the company.

Not having a handle on the culture and infrastructure when introducing something new can be deadly to many businesses.

---

28   Henrik Kniberg, and Anders Ivarsson, "Scaling Agile @ Spotify," October 2012, accessed October 27, 2018, https://blog.crisp.se/wp-content/uploads/2012/11/SpotifyScaling.pdf.

Take Starbucks's ill-advised foray into the Australian market in the early 2000s. It expanded quickly without having a full understanding of the "down under" coffee culture and its tastes, and bypassed market research. By 2008, the company closed nearly three-quarters of its locations, racking up $105 million in losses.[29]

Spotify was a unique company in a unique situation. Yes, seeing success and growth as a threat to its start-up mentality had been an issue before, and since, but the company itself is one of a kind, as is its product and customers. It's kind of like snowflakes: looked at from far away they seem quite similar, but at close scale, they're all beautifully different.

As a dolphin does when it peers into a mirror and recognizes what is unique about it, and how it can change, Spotify did enough internal analysis to figure out what kind of customized approach would work for it. It was a company that saw who it was, and made its self-awareness lead to an individualized, tailored route to success.

Other companies have their own agile models that work for their own unique situations. Tesla brought iterative deployments to auto manufacturing, rolling out both simple dashboard elements and fundamental handling elements for regular download. And as opposed to the standard annual release of new automobiles, Tesla began showcasing new products quarterly.[30]

As Spotify did, Amazon modified a scrum approach to its application of agile. Though there were underpinnings of agile-like behavior at the end of the millennium for the behemoth, its software engineering teams began transitioning to scrum almost organically

---

29 Ashley Turner, "Why There Are Almost No Starbucks in Australia," CNBC, July 25, 2018, accessed October 26, 2018, https://www.cnbc.com/2018/07/20/starbucks-australia-coffee-failure.html.

30 Steve Blank, "Tesla and Adobe: Why Continuous Deployment May Mean Continuous Customer Disappointment," Forbes, January 3, 2014, accessed October 27, 2018, https://www.forbes.com/sites/steveblank/2014/01/03/tesla-and-adobe-why-continuous-deployment-may-mean-continuous-customer-disappointment/#60218bab13bc.

between 2004 and 2009, and it spread from there. While there wasn't any management-level order for widespread adoption, smaller groups took on decentralized autonomy, champions began naturally proselytizing to other employees, and only after it caught on were dedicated roles created. So, its enactment of scrum was a natural occurrence with no oversight, initially.

None of these companies can be emulated in how they adopted and adapted an agile approach. They had their own people who worked together in their own way, and their histories shaped how they would act.

This is where and why your organization has to create its own path and act like a dolphin. Do the internal investigation and begin on a path of knowing yourself. The first thing your company has to do when seeing which kind of agile methodology it can tailor to fit its needs is evaluate holistically how the business is currently set up. What are the problems it's trying to solve? What are its strengths and weaknesses? Where is it already acting like a smoothly efficient, autonomous, communicative, customer-first agile machine? Is the technology there, how's the automation, and what roles are people filling?

We've seen that establishing the culture is important, but so is making sure an infrastructure is in place for such a big transition. Before we start implementing SAFe for a company that has no testing automation set up, we'd want to devote a significant amount of resources to set that up. For an organization that has a weak product management group, before focusing on the software engineers, we might want to work on training new POs and PMs in understanding principles before getting off to the races.

There are many consultants who do little more than read off stereo instructions when undertaking the incredibly difficult job of helping transform a company to an agile approach. Without taking stock of where a company is, they're just forcing square pegs into round holes, no matter the shape of the peg. They don't know the principles, so they're bound by the rules. If SAFe says that a train delivers a potentially shippable increment (PSI) every ten weeks, they're beholden to that rule because they don't understand the *reasoning* behind it. Even if a company works better having that time-box be slightly longer, the by-the-book consultant won't be swayed.

That's a shame. They—and you too—have to take the time to individualize the model to your company. When consultants don't truly understand the principles of agile, and the fact that it's based on the empirical process, they lose the forest for the trees. Without understanding *why* scrum teams should be anywhere from three to nine people, they don't think about the need too deeply and just mandate that no teams should be more than nine. Even when there's a large organization that really needs those units to be eleven or twelve at the beginning, the purist consultants will be immovable.

Customizing agile methodologies often comes down to constraints, and oversight of the transition should consider the organization's unique position and relationships. One of my clients was an old company, a large monolith that had numerous applications so tightly wound together with the underlying code that each part was inextricable from the other. If engineers wanted to make an upgrade or patch to one part, they'd have to test the whole thing for quality; an alteration in one small aspect could prevent users from logging in. That's a bad pre-existing condition when it comes to the needs of continuous deployment and testing, and it's something I suggested we spend focused time and resources on. Forging ahead without taking that necessary detour from the agile "stereo instructions" would have absolutely hurt the company in the long term.

Spotify had its own issues when establishing what its tailored approach would be. It was growing quickly and had to keep modifying to fit the workforce, which was constantly expanding and dividing into new teams. It also didn't nail it on the first shot: A lag in deployment execution by the operations team led agile leadership to transfer the deployments over to the software engineering team, which ended up being a huge time saver.[31] It was easy for Spotify to make this kind of maneuver because it had already established a built-in high standard of autonomy and transparency, as well as inter-team trust. Copying Spotify's model by the numbers won't work for many other organizations.

There are also differences between industries that are important to recognize and come with certain constraints. In chapter 7, I mentioned the Pixar cofounder Ed Catmull, who advocates embracing failure as a means of learning and growing. That's very important! Agile embraces failure, realizing that customer feedback from those mistakes can lead to a much better product. But even Catmull admits that "there are arenas … in which a zero failure rate is essential," listing commercial airlines, hospitals, and banks as sectors where failure would be devastatingly bad. [32] This is another case in which an "out of the box" methodology that's pushing for failure and feedback would have severe ramifications without some adaptations along the way.

Tailoring approaches to fit an organization needs to work at both the industry level and the company level. Executives are often guilty of believing that what works at one company will work at another. Marissa Mayer, one of Google's first employees, was heavily

---

31   Jeff Sutherland, "Spotify's Secret for Competing with Apple, Amazon, and Google," Openview, January 23, 2014, access October 27, 2018, http://labs.openviewpartners.com/spotify-great-agile-example-scrum-done-right/#.W9Ix_hNKjfa.

32   Ed Catmull, with Amy Wallace, *Creativity, Inc.*, New York: Random House, 2014, p. 115.

entrenched in that culture and tried to imitate its management style when she became Yahoo CEO in 2012. Mayer said adoringly of Larry Page and Sergey Brin that they "just yelled at us until we became what they needed us to become, and get done what they needed to be done. And so I said, 'Look, I'm going to just rinse and repeat that, hopefully with less yelling.'"[33]

That technique didn't match well with Yahoo's employees, who noted low morale among the departments. Mayer was out in 2017.

Just as copying and pasting culture doesn't work from company to company, copying an agile methodology won't either. Taking the time to know yourself is key to finding an approach that will jive with your organization with some tweaks. Evaluate your company on what needs to be improved from a cultural or personal standpoint, and what capabilities need to be upgraded; set up training for new roles and those new ideas; identify roadblocks and obstructions; and initiate a pilot program with a team that's uniquely well suited. Get feedback, reflect, and improve on that iteration.

Just as copying and pasting culture doesn't work from company to company, copying an agile methodology won't either. Taking the time to know yourself is key to finding an approach that will jive with your organization with some tweaks.

Each company and each team will have different needs, and the way you (and consultants) should handle that will change.

---

33   Shana Lebowitz, "Marissa Mayer Says Her Google Bosses 'Yelled at Us until We Became What They Needed Us to Become'—and It Wasn't a Bad Thing," *Business Insider,* April 21, 2018, accessed October 28, 2018, https://www.businessinsider.com/yahoo-marissa-mayer-copied-google-management-style-2018-4.

This concept is also important for a company in various stages of growth, as well as teams in various stages of growth. The processes and structure that work for a company after a year of significant expansion and hiring will be different from what worked for them the prior year. Divisions within a company may also be at drastically opposite ends of engineering. A new digital group versus an old business unit in the same organization will probably each require differently tailored approaches, but at the same time, that new digital group can't emulate a digital group from *another* company.

The point is to pay attention to where the company, as a whole, and the specific divisions are, and treat them all as unique. Not all of the technical improvements and training sequences may be necessary, depending on the team or organization. I've worked with a company whose engineers were all intricately conversant with one centralized tracking tool. So, I was able to skip that part of the implementation and move on. On the other hand, I've been with a company where twenty-nine teams were using twenty-nine different tracking systems; you better believe I had to work on just standardizing that for three months.

Often there's a role issue within companies that needs specific and personalized attention. New positions need to be well established before implementing a roadmap to any unique methodology. Companies that don't have strong product management groups will need time to get training, especially if they're trying to move business analysts into PO roles. Analysts are experts in the field, used to providing answers after in-depth investigation and analysis, and building detailed requirements. On the other hand, POs are more about asking questions of the customer and getting feedback, rather than providing answers to the business side. At the onset of working toward an agile approach, you may need consultants to spend six to nine months working with the product management group, wrapping their minds around new responsibilities as well as concepts such as the minimum viable product.

As with so many things in the agile approach, tailoring your company's methodology comes down to trust. There needs to be both intra- and inter-team trust and accountability, and there needs to be top-down trust and accountability as well. That's one of the hardest psychological changes for leadership to fully internalize.

It's incredibly easy for executives to *nominally* get on board with the company's transformation to agile, not really understanding what it asks of them, let alone what the principles are. And as we've seen, there are a number of intentional or unintentional roadblocks they can use to halt the agile methodology from being effectively planted. At the beginning, they may declare, "Sure, bring on agile!" But as the transformation takes hold, hard choices need to help coerce it along. Too often, we see management trying to alter agile methodologies to help fit the company, instead of the other way around.

As Ed Catmull points out, it's important to let mistakes happen (in most sectors), so companies can learn and grow from those opportunities. But the fear of mistakes can drive leadership to micromanage and resist full autonomy. Hard choices come with transitions. We learn from trial and error, just as Spotify continued to hone and perfect. We have to maintain a psychologically safe environment for team members to fail.

Consultants peddling a cookie-cutter implementation, be it SAFe, scrum, or any other framework, can also be the downfall of an agile transformation. This is doubly dangerous because not only does it waste the company's time, effort, and money, but it also reinforces the notion that agile methodologies won't work and gives skeptical managers a reason to throw up their hands and say, "Well, we tried."

Examine any company successfully working with an agile methodology and you'll see one that knows itself and what its strengths and weaknesses are. You'll find a company that went through learning curves to arrive at a model that worked for it. Whatever modifications were instituted were the product of its knowing what its capabilities were and how best to adjust the workflow for the optimal quality, efficiency, and predictability of continuous deployments. Good consultants will uncover those traits of your company and help customize your roadmap to success.

And as we'll see in the next chapter, it begins with little steps.

Examine any company successfully working with an agile methodology and you'll see one that knows itself and what its strengths and weaknesses are.

Chapter 10

DON'T LET PERFECT GET IN THE WAY OF GOOD ENOUGH

I've been a consultant for almost two decades. For a good portion of that time, I prided myself on having the solutions for my clients. I thought they appreciated me for this, but it took me over fifteen years to embrace where my value actually comes from. I've realized that the *organization* has the answers, and my job is to ask the right questions to lead my clients there. Bar none, the hardest lesson for me has been to subdue the part of my brain that wants to do all the work and find the information for my clients by myself. It's been difficult! Over the years, I've talked to people in different industries who approach me about problems within their companies, how things aren't working correctly, how responsibilities aren't clear, and so on. Everything pushes me to find the right answers and come up with *the* definitive list of how they should right their ships.

But that's not what they really needed. What they needed was someone to pose key questions and help them know themselves so they could see what should be adjusted, what required facilitation, and what demanded a change in course—and also what was workable.

It's no different for software engineering. The best kind of leadership and workflow operates in less defined circles, ones that appreciate open-ended communication, flexibility, and trial balloons. We're dealing with an empirical process, asking for a constant flow of transparency, inspection, and adaptation.

For much of my career, my technique was akin to a waterfall approach. As business analysts are, I was trained to be the infallible expert. Companies operated linearly, and so did I. I gave my clients my definitive research and answers, and similarly, waterfall methodology relies on sprawling, upfront documentation with little input along the way from the people it impacts. A ton of focus is placed on gathering information about the project, the scope, and the result *way* down the line. Business analysts compiling all of this data speak for the customer and translate all of that into requirements that are delivered down the road to the next step in system design.

Simply put, in waterfall, all of this documentation sets up the very strict blueprint for the final deployment. These business requirement documents (BRDs) are supposed to be all-encompassing, covering everything and the kitchen sink during the project, spanning deployments that could happen up to eighteen months down the road. Every single requirement is outlined, every *i* dotted and every *t* crossed. Once these BRDs are created, they're handed over to system analysts, who convert them into FRDs—functional requirement documents—which are essentially the *how* in this equation: *Here's how those business requirements will be answered.* The analysts, here, are the subject matter experts. They have an in-depth sense of the system so they're creating tremendous Word documents with very, very detailed specifications.

If you're working at one of these large companies that demand this metric ton of upfront documentation, you're well aware how comprehensive these documents are and how they try to cover every possible contingency, such that the project itself seems unwieldy and arbitrary when looking at things so far in the future. This is partly to avoid finger pointing down the line in case something that wasn't unaccounted for suddenly appears. The typical blame culture will always look for the person who dropped the ball in requirements gathering.

The MVP Starts the Learning Process

Just as I had to reimagine my role as a consultant and how I would fit into making an organization the strongest and most flexible it could be for a modernized industry, a company has to reimagine the role of its analysts, managers, and product team when working to create the best product for its customers. In a manufacturing world of a defined process and waterfall approach, analysts step in for the customers, creating BRDs and FRDs to assume the needs of future end users. But while the analysts claim to be experts in the field, they can't possibly predict changing requirements, commonplace with software engineering and rapidly advancing technology. Those changing requirements represent a big problem for the calcified upfront documentation. Requesting alterations to the project once it's in progress is both difficult and painful.

Agile seeks to change all of that. And by "all of that," I don't mean the workflow and process alone, but how we conceive the product, how leadership fits into the company, how the analysts operate, how product management interfaces, and even what role the end user plays. This requires a big shift in company and employee mind-sets. It involves trust and delegation, collaboration, and acceptance of feedback, letting go, and understanding that: *Hey, we're not in waterfall anymore, Dorothy.*

One of the many downfalls of the waterfall methodology is the high probability of failure and waste when it comes to an eighteen-month-long software engineering project. It's not just that requirements change; demand shifts and the technology landscape advances. Smaller steps toward final releases are advisable to save both money and labor.

In his seminal book on entrepreneurship and innovation, *The Lean Start-Up*, Eric Ries popularized the term *minimum viable product* (MVP), which he defines as "that version of a new product which allows a team to collect the maximum amount of validated learning about customers with the least effort."[34] Ries adds that "contrary to traditional product engineering, which usually involves a long, thoughtful incubation period and strives for product perfection, the goal of the MVP is to begin the process of learning, not end it."[35]

The MVP turns product planning and data gathering on their heads. As opposed to aggregating a ludicrous amount of data and analysis and churning out a tome of epic proportions before designing a product that nobody wants to buy, the MVP is a sort of a trial balloon, one that has just enough features to satisfy early customers

---

34 Eric Ries, "Minimum Viable Product: A Guide," *Startup Lessons Learned*, blog, August 3, 2009, accessed November 2, 2018, http://www.startuplessonslearned.com/2009/08/minimum-viable-product-guide.html.

35 Eric Ries, *The Lean Startup*, New York: Penguin Books, 2011, p. 93.

and provide feedback for future product engineering.

Facebook, for instance, uses a quasi-continuous delivery model at scale to incorporate its teams' *canary* deployments, small software testing that reaches only a small group of users, allowing for contained testing and feedback and side-by-side administrating and reporting.[36] This allows Facebook to see how viable its software is with routine experimentation and reaction before adjusting and deploying to the majority of users (or shutting it down).

As a concept, MVP has been misunderstood and bastardized. Some software engineers use it as a weapon to chop scope off a product backlog. The engineers may not want to work on all of the requirements of a product, and just pick and choose what the top features are that they'll tackle, and then call that the MVP. In actuality, it's not a tool for software engineers; it's one for product management. Ries says, "It is inadequate to build a prototype that is evaluated solely for internal quality by engineers and designers. We also need to get it in front of potential customers to gauge their reactions."[37]

It's all about the feedback. It's the product management team having a hunch that if they sell this product, people will buy it. They're not 100 percent certain yet, so why spend all this money building the best version of it right out of the gate? Instead, they'll build a version that they can test. It's the cheapest, easiest, quickest way they'll have a viable product to validate whether the hunch was right. *It won't be perfect, but it'll be good enough to let the team know if they should either continue developing it, or kill it.*

As Ries adds, "Minimum viable products range in complexity from extremely simple smoke tests (little more than advertisement)

---

36 Hrishikesh Barua, "How Facebook Achieves Rapid Release at Massive Scale," InfoQueue, September 7, 2017, accessed November 2, 2018, https://www.infoq.com/news/2017/09/facebook-release-scale.

37 Eric Ries, *The Lean Startup* (New York: Penguin Books, 2011), p. 76.

to actual early prototypes complete with problems and missing features."[38] Facebook's canary releases are generally small functionality alterations for consumers: if the customer doesn't like them, they don't see the light of day through production. This changes depending on the context, of course. For example, when banks that have large companies (or even countries) as their consumers that require the highest quality in order to process trillions of dollars in transactions daily, small functionality alterations can't be thrown into the mix as trial balloons.

But for other organizations, the whole point of the MVP is to start the learning process. That process doesn't come from the analyst, who was responsible in the waterfall model for being the in-house expert, or from management or the software engineers. It comes from the customer, with whom you're in collaboration to create a high quality product for total satisfaction.

Shifting Roles of the PM and PO

The MVP shows the importance of the product team, and in agile, the shifting roles reflect that. While smaller companies combine the PM and PO—space and budgetary constraints generally require this to be the same person—larger organizations operating in an agile methodology separate the two and give each defined responsibilities.

PMs really have the customer-facing role. Many in the industry think of them as the product *marketing* manager. They act as the liaison between sales and marketing and the product team. PMs own the blueprint for the product and control the prioritized product backlog. They're able to relay information and the functionality of the product to the marketing teams, executives, and even the customers.

POs require a lot of collaboration in their roles as well. If the

---

38   Ibid., p. 95.

PM is the *why*, setting the vision for the overall strategy, then the PO is the *what*, conveying feedback through user stories to the software engineers and coming up with solutions in close consultation with the software engineers. Engineers, testers and other non-PO members of the team are the *how*, making it happen and putting it into the product.

Converting from a waterfall to agile approach asks for a mental shift for both PMs and POs. PMs move from market research and writing meticulous BRDs to writing features or epics in different formats, prioritizing backlogs, setting out the vision for the product, and working with both customer-facing departments, such as marketing and sales, and software engineering. A PM's role expands, and it's no small feat to keep up with the new responsibilities.

It's a heavy transition to PO as well. Under waterfall, business or system analysts are accustomed to gathering requirements and writing the FRDs, being treated as the subject matter experts in the company, and issuing massive documentation that outlines every piece of functionality. In agile, they're being asked to have a conversation with the engineers, based on feedback from the customer or PM. They take the epics or features from the PMs, and break those down into user stories.

There's a functional as well as philosophical change for both POs and PMs in agile: Their identity shifts from being "the answer man" to being "the question man," as I did in consulting. This is hard to internalize, and often difficult for the former analyst to adapt to easily.

Much as I did with my own hang-ups about moving from being a consultant with all the answers to someone just asking the right questions, business or system analysts moving to either a PM or PO role have to subdue an ego and learn a brand-new talent: how to communicate and facilitate. Transitioning from writing all-inclusive requirement documentation to writing features, epics, or user stories takes practice and acceptance. POs, and in a scaled environment, PMs, have to move from being the subject matter expert and assuming what the customers need to actually finding out what they want—and basing solutions and discussions on that quick feedback loop that comes with iterative deployment.

Some companies seeking to fill these new agile roles of PMs and POs hire from outside the firm, but trying to hire, in some cases, a hundred positions, and having that amount of turnover, just isn't feasible. Educating the analysts in workshops and training sessions is a must, but there's also a lot of trial-by-fire experience that needs to be a part of the process. The new responsibilities for a PM and PO—actually composing the epics, features, or user stories, instead of the detailed functional requirement documents that they've been laboring over for fifteen years, for example—takes a new skills toolkit.

The user story generally comes in this form: *As a [user], I need to [action] so that [beneficial reason]*. The example we saw in chapter 5—"As a *bank teller*, I need to *query customers' accounts* so that *I can tell them what their balances are*"—shows the simplicity of the language. But as simple as it may seem, it takes a lot of practice. It's not about perfecting the language; it's about the collaboration, that shared communication between the PM or PO, the customer, and the software engineers. There are always three *C*s to a user story:

The card: the promise to open up that dialogue.

The conversation: the collaboration between the team and PO.

The confirmation: the assurance that the card is complete and the task is considered done/the need is filled.

Yielding the unofficial title of "subject matter expert" to the customer is difficult, but the required collaboration that fulfills these three *Cs* is not to be disregarded in its complexity either. Instead of working in a relative vacuum, accumulating research, and writing functional requirements, POs should now be sitting next to software engineers and working on finding solutions *with* them to create the best product that will satisfy the user stories. This new coerced teamwork of PO and software engineer can be awkward. In the previous waterfall model, the two would interact, but only in small doses, not in the 24/7 dialogue that agile demands.

Working this way requires a more flexible attitude toward creation of the product: instead of giving directives that say, for instance, "the blue button will be on the upper right hand side of the page," the PO will now need to engage in a more open-ended way that offers the software engineers an opportunity to find the solution.

It also asks the product team not to let the quest for perfection get in the way of the *good enough*. Because of the continuous deployments and need for adaptability, not every question will be answered from the get-go. This acceptance of the unknown can be a startling pivot. The fear of blame culture, where a mistake could lead to somebody getting yelled at down the road, can drive former analysts crazy. But they have to overcome the urge to force a more wide-ranging product. The mistakes can be extremely beneficial because customers' feedback is an integral part of the workflow and improvements.

I only came to grips with this after a decade and a half in the space—and, likewise, these new PMs and POs also have to accept the fact that *they're not the experts*. The customers know better than anyone in the company what they want. Now, we

The customers know better than anyone in the company what they want. Now, we have to interface with them and get that valuable information.

have to interface with them and get that valuable information from that communication, not from "siloing up" and researching. This is agile, and the customer conversations rule.

The Planning Onion

While documentation is greatly reduced in this new approach to product development, it's not—despite rumors and fear-mongering—eliminated altogether. Agile prizes working software over comprehensive documentation, but that doesn't mean it's tossed out the window, wholesale. As I covered in the myths section of chapter 2, necessary and valuable documentation is always important. Needless and wasteful documentation that will likely change is a drain on resources. The features and user stories provide a product backlog that's open-ended and allows input from the software engineers along the way, as well as the flexibility to incorporate feedback from the customer.

Similarly, planning isn't disregarded either. If anything, planning plays a *more* important role over the course of software engineering, but not in the same way as in waterfall, where planning meetings revolve around BRD and FRD reviews. Short-term planning is necessary and prevalent within agile. The problem is, with iterative deployments, a lot of people have the misconception that short-term planning is *all* there is. Under agile, it's a more holistic planning that deals with the granular but also the macro-objectives, not only of the product but also of the company's strategy.

Think of an onion: Each layer gets smaller as you cut deeper in. A popular image, and one that causes far fewer tears thankfully, is the agile onion: six layers depicting different levels of planning. On the outside is the big layer, the one wrapping around all the others, known as *strategic* planning. It's a three-, five-, or ten-year plan: *What business are we in and whom do we compete with? Where are we, as an organization, headed?*

Inside that is the second-largest layer, the *portfolio* layer: *What products at large do our customers need? What group of products will work together to solidify the vision of the organization?* The third layer is *product* planning: *What capabilities does the product need? How can the specific product evolve in the future?*

Inside the three outermost layers are the three interior ones. The fourth circle is *release* planning, giving an overview of work roughly every three months. Release planning can give the scope of work for the next three months as well as the resources and time frame demanded of it. One level below is *iteration* planning that occurs at the beginning of every time box. The very last inner layer is the *day* layer, incorporating those team meetings that occur on a daily basis—some form of stand-up in which team members discuss what they've completed, what they're working on, and what's blocking them, coordinating their efforts.

While most agile teams are concerned with only the three innermost layers (iteration, release, and day), you can see that the company as a whole has a structure for staying focused on all six to present a comprehensive way of thinking about not only the release but the product's evolution, the group it fits into, and the company's landscape.

Between the change in documentation and planning, the shift in responsibilities, and the transformation of product to a more iterative state of release, there's a large psychological shift for employees. They have to let go of their old traditions of working and thinking, something that's uncomfortable for them because they've been doing something a certain way for years and likely were trained in it. Managers have to become leaders, moving from command-

and-control to inspiring, coaching, and facilitating; analysts have to move from knowing the answers to asking questions, from providing the data to opening the conversation.

As your teams work on letting go, it's also important to remind them to let go of *the perfect*. Don't let it get in the way of the *good enough*. The software engineers and product management team have to move past the hyperprecise guidelines that predict exactly what the product will look like a year and a half down the road. They need to internalize the reality that there's a lot of unknown—and that's okay! Feedback and customer collaboration are important ingredients to make the best-quality software. Nobody knows what the customer wants better than the customer.

We can prize individuals and interactions by putting the PO next to the software engineers for face time and real communication. We can prize working software by first pushing out a minimum viable product to gauge the customer's reaction, and then striving, in every iteration, to make it better. We can prize customer collaboration by receiving feedback and comments and implementing them in future deployments. We can respond to change by being flexible in our workflow to allow for it in the first place. And in this way, we can live up to the agile manifesto in small, incremental, rapid steps.

Software engineering is a different beast from manufacturing. The approach that the industry started with was a good mechanism, but it's misapplied here. And now we have to undo a lot of that misapplication and implement a new way to conceive the entire workflow.

Chapter 11

DO YOU HAVE THE RIGHT TOOLS IN PLACE?

We've covered a lot of what it takes to prepare a company for the implementation of an agile approach:

- knowing yourself, what practices you use today, and how they can be improved;

- how important it is to make sure everyone is on the same page in what agile is looking to accomplish with the business, and get buy-in from the top down;

- how much it will take to change the mind-set and old traditions of the organization and its employees;

- how the culture has to be ripe for a new methodology;

- how the personnel has to operate as productive, self-managed, transparent teams.

And now it's time to bring in a consultant (like me) to help run educational sessions, coordinate everybody with a congruous tracking tool, and—

Hold up. Slow down. Hiring a consultant to help implement a new agile framework with iterative planning and deployments has to go hand-in-hand with examining and, if necessary, improving your infrastructure. If the infrastructure for your software engineering isn't designed and built to support continuous integration and continuous deployment (CI/CD), and your tools are equally lacking, this needs to be addressed. Consider making technical upgrades to your underlying system while your people are getting upgrades to their *own* knowledge through tracking work, process redefinition, and other forms of training. Ideally, the timing of tool readiness and organization readiness will align.

There's going to be a lot of effort and time spent in training. There'll be cost in personnel turnover and in briefly disrupting the engineering chain. People will be upset, uncertain, and disoriented at the beginning. So, if you're going to go through all of this, you'll want to make sure you're getting *all* that agile can offer: quicker, more predictable, high-quality software, and its ancillary benefits, such as a happier, more productive workplace and fully satisfied customers. And if you really want to fully reap those benefits, you ought to make sure the infrastructure and tools are in place as the teams are trained in how to support and use them. If you don't have the computing and automation infrastructure empowering your software engineering team, they'll never realize the full benefits an agile methodology can bring. Put another way, it'll be the equivalent of flying the *Mil-*

lennium Falcon but never jumping to light speed. Nice enough ship, but don't you want to realize *all* of the benefits?

We all know that upgrading your capabilities will take money and time, but it's worth it. Companies need to be deploying iteratively to keep up with the quick cycles, technological advancements, and changing customer needs. Making sure your pipeline for workflow is quick and responsive by integrating automated tools with continuous delivery into the infrastructure is central to making this happen.

Continuous Integration, Continuous Deployment

Continuous integration (CI) and continuous deployment (CD) are the lifeblood of an agile organization that's able to deliver quality software predictably and with ample speed. CI is "the process of automating the build and testing of code every time a team member commits changes to version control. CI encourages software engineers to frequently share their code and unit tests by merging their changes into a shared version control repository after every small task completion. Committing code triggers an automated build system."[39] CD is the automated, consistent method of pushing that integrated code into production.

CI/CD provides a consistent, repeatable, and automated pipeline for integrating, building, testing, and deploying applications all the way through production in a controlled and safe manner. The speed and efficiency of an agile software engineering approach depends on this capability: A continuous and automated workflow that provides short feedback loops for software engineers to iterate and swiftly deliver new features to production. The pipeline allows for small, contained changes and improvements with multiple deployments a

---

39   Sam Guckenheimer, "What is Continuous Integration?" Microsoft, April 3, 2017, accessed January 10, 2019, https://docs.microsoft.com/en-us/azure/devops/learn/what-is-continuous-integration.

day, regularly upgrading the end user's experience.

Beyond automating the integration, build, and deployment of code, an efficient CI/CD pipeline provides many other benefits including reducing or eliminating downtime for environments, and automated, continuous, consistent testing to catch bugs early in the process. There's also immediate clarity on code quality. Additionally, CI/CD facilitates communication between software engineers and POs, allowing for more frequent testing by users and therefore better feedback, with smaller chunks of feature sets put in production for customers. Continuous, fast, small improvements delivered safely to production is what the agile approach demands for success. CI/CD greatly shortens the lead time from request to production and addresses what is generally the biggest speed bump in software engineering.

The speed and efficiency of an agile software engineering approach depends on a continuous and automated workflow that provides short feedback loops for software engineers to iterate and swiftly deliver new features to production.

Sounds pretty good, huh? It is! So, how can you construct this smooth-flowing pipeline for your organization? Traditional operations and technology organizations that continue to practice waterfall are unlikely to have the proper architecture, infrastructure, and tools to support this. These organizations tend toward siloed teams with rigid boundaries and interaction based on process-heavy contracts that result in slow progress and inefficient communications between teams. The resource cost, not to mention the necessary slow-down that comes with building the new foundation may be difficult for leadership to approve.

(Re)building the foundation takes upfront investment to make it all operational. Invest the time, money, and effort now so that, down the road, you'll be able to build and deliver new features quickly and cleanly, your deployments will be faster and more consistent and predictable, and you'll spend fewer resources on debugging and waiting for delivery. Think of it as Lasik eye surgery for your company's weak eyesight. Undergoing it may be costly, and recovery can take time, but the payoff is substantial, and it makes life a lot easier.

Dev Ops

There has been a fairly standard operating procedure of engineering and deployment for larger companies, at least until the dev ops revolution of the last decade. In traditional companies, there's a handoff with work: code is written by software engineers, tested by QA, packaged up, and handed off to operations, which deploys and runs it despite having little to no investment in, knowledge of, or influence on the end result. This siloed nature between creation and deployment is not ideal. Not only does it cause frustration for software engineers and operations personnel, but it also leads to slowness, communications problems, poor design and implementation, and ultimately, significant challenges with the run of the application, which negatively affects the customers' satisfaction.

Dev ops seeks to rectify this. The portmanteau of the two departments is the "practice of operations and development engineers participating together in the entire service lifecycle, from design through the development process to production support."[40] This concept

---

40   Ernest Mueller, "What Is DevOps?" *The Agile Admin,* blog, revised July 24, 2017, accessed January 10, 2018, https://theagileadmin.com/what-is-devops/.

improves the relationship within the organization by advocating better communication and collaboration between software engineering and operations, and also addresses the bottlenecked workflow. And perhaps most pertinent to agile, it creates a short feedback loop over the course of the design/build/deploy/run process that results in a better designed and deployed product.

By eliminating the code handoff, dev ops unites two teams as one and gives them a shared goal. Software engineers understand operation's needs and can design for them upfront (improving delivery and support), and operations becomes invested in the end product. By integrating the two teams, collaboration, transparency, and productivity are increased.

The practice of dev ops fits perfectly into the agile approach. With a strong CI/CD foundation, software engineers and operations can collaborate and communicate efficiently and effectively to deliver product to market in an iterative fashion. The smaller, bite-sized deployments of feature sets can provide consistent, informed feedback to continually improve and innovate.

But none of it is possible with the swiftness we desire out of CI/CD without that underlying infrastructure and tools that can take care of building, testing, managing, and tracking.

Tools for such purposes have, predictably, flooded the market, bringing with them a wonderful simplicity—such as pushing a Staples Easy Button and setting a hundred tasks into motion. And this means that there isn't a siloed team in tech operations managing all of this anymore. Agile and its processes are able to identify roadblocks and lags and eliminate (or at least mitigate) them. Allowing software engineering and operations to work together is appealing as it can shorten process time and churn out deployments more rapidly. So, which infrastructure changes and which tools can help the organization create the most effective CI/CD pipeline?

Multiple Environments

Right off the bat, your organization is going to need a software-defined infrastructure that can manage the environments for your software engineers, treating configuration-as-code. As a start, however, you need to have a set of environments that allows the pipeline of engineering work to easily flow from a software engineer's laptop to production. When software engineers are working on different features, they often operate in isolation from each other, typically on their own laptop with an environment that is like, but not the same as, the production environment. For obvious reasons, you don't want your software engineers to be working in the production environment. Fiddling around with new code where the actual application is live is a recipe for disaster, as it can lead to outages, stability issues, and potential catastrophe that may require hours, if not days, to resolve.

In a traditional environment model, organizations have their software engineers working in multiple fixed and permanent environments that feed each other. While organizations attempt to make each environment the same as production, this is often not possible. Environment drift, which occurs when configurations slightly diverge because changes aren't tracked or maintained in any comprehensive way and flow as code through the same pipeline, happens over time without dev ops.

Multiple environments are a great idea. Having environments capable of being provisioned on demand for any purpose (such as running multiple tests at one time) is even better. It allows a multitude of work to occur concurrently, making sure everyone's staying productive. It also fosters innovation and eliminates lags and downtime in making updates to the software, saving the company time and money. But your organization has to ensure that the copies being used in different environments by engineers can be reintegrated with one another. Pipelines that monitor your source control repository, and automatically integrate software engineer code manage this.

Version control and code branching strategies are necessary for teams to work simultaneously on separate facets of a program for greater efficiency. Multiple copies of the code are made and shared with the different teams, which can make their necessary changes without disrupting the main active version. With proper branching and merging, code is integrated, tested, and merged into the main branch, where it's promoted to production. All of this means that software engineers can work in a collaborative environment and attack different tasks, minimizing the risk of disrupting each other and negatively impacting higher environments. With this approach, it makes sense to merge code routinely and in small chunks, in order to make debugging easier. This ensures that defects will decrease, and through an automated pipeline, code will move faster and more predictably through to production.

The advent of the cloud has allowed for these multiple environments as well. There are also advantages to having your environments hosted with a cloud provider, including a better replication of production and never having to bother with setting up local machines. Cloud-based environments are transient, allowing environments as needed to be "spun up" and "torn down" on demand.

Agile depends on feedback from end users and stakeholders to keep the product geared toward satisfying clients and developing useful add-ons. Agile operates on that continual dialogue between customer and company—and getting information about the software from the actual people who use it is integral to the process. If your teams are operating in multiple environments, incorporating user feedback and altering the code to satisfy concerns can happen quickly. CI/CD speeds up feedback by automating the processes of build and deploy through multiple environments.

Software engineers can work in a development environment, isolated from QA testing in a QA environment, and isolated from end users reviewing tests. You can receive feedback without putting the new feature in the master branch, instead pushing the test product to a select group (e.g., POs) and then adjusting accordingly before every user sees the alterations. In the more transparent world of agile, where face-to-face communication and, in some frameworks, daily stand-ups are the norm, a software engineer may receive necessary feedback before the code even sees the light of day at the end of the iteration.

Agile operates on that continual dialogue between customer and company— and getting information about the software from the actual people who use it is integral to the process.

The feedback loop—the detailed feedback that can come throughout the span of a software engineering life cycle—is necessary during CI/CD. Automatic monitoring and tracking, unit tests, and code review are all things that could be implemented in your organization to aid software engineering, but you have to take the time and energy to set them up. There's enormous value that comes from the short feedback loop via an automated tool that allows a team to receive immediate positive and negative feedback on the integrity of the code. Building a pipeline that will enable coding, testing, and building at the same time is a huge lever for organizations looking to shorten lead time.

Automation Tools

There are a number of tools that help initiate and oversee the CI/CD aspects that will promote and aid iterative deployment. Jenkins, a popular open-source server that manages and aids in builds and tests via pipelines that dev ops creates, is a great example. It's one of several CI tools that define and orchestrate the pipeline for building, testing, and packaging; it can deploy code rapidly without manual intervention and generate quick feedback reports. Teams can then get the best out of their workflow, making them collaborative and transparent, recalling the three pillars of the empirical process: transparency (keeping everything visible), inspection (reviewing the product and process), and adaptation (continually improving).

Automation platforms that can help with configuration management are also powerful tools for organizations moving toward an agile approach. Configuration management applications make sure that new machines are set up as they ought to be—with the right software and configuration, where consistency is maintained and managed from a central location. Tools such as Chef, which can provision and manage servers by transforming infrastructure into code, are particularly helpful for software engineers in creating multiple environments to build and test in. (Chef takes the culinary analogy to its logical extreme, calling each server setup a "recipe," with a number of those recipes gathered together comprising a "cookbook," each of which concerns single tasks within the process. There are also "knives," "kitchens," and "supermarkets," naturally— no "Bobby Flay" tool available just yet.)

Following applications such as Jenkins, which enables teams to create pipelines that build and test continuously as well as generate feedback loops, and Chef, which can help manage and recreate servers and environments, are automated tools that provide oversight for the source code. For example, GitHub facilitates the management, tracking, changes, and merging of code. All of these applications, together, are able to reduce the manual and highly error-prone grunt work in the pipeline, leaving engineers free to do what they do best: create.

It's important, however, to keep on top of support of the tools and infrastructure. As much as concepts behind agile continue to adapt and grow, so, too, do those tools. They need to be maintained continuously or the pipeline can show its age and your processes will fall behind the competition.

Putting It All Together

Much of the work preparing your organization for repairs to a bad agile implementation, or a transition to it in the first place, revolves around the culture, mind-set, personalities, and knowledge of the company's processes. Those are incredibly important, and agile won't work in a business not adequately set up for it, mentally. Agile will *also* not work in a business not set up for it, physically. Having automated tools in place, ensuring the CI/CD pipeline is effective and attended to, and committing to the dev ops practice are three major steps your organization needs to take to create an infrastructure the agile process can love.

It's certainly easier for start-ups, operating without the overhead, complex departments, and traditional "ways of doing things," to be flexible, and from the get-go, embrace the notion of dev ops. But larger companies can do it, too, and be just as nimble as start-ups. And that's where we turn our attention next.

Chapter 12

HOW CAN YOU BE JUST AS AGILE AS A START-UP?

Galapagos tortoises may not understand why they need to be as self-aware and socially active as dolphins. After all, things have been working just fine for them until now. They've been around for a long time, can survive up to a year without food or water, and enjoy relaxing and snoozing for around sixteen hours a day.

Old enterprise companies may ask themselves that same question. They have a lot working for them: a history of success, job security, deep pockets, and a steady stock price. But there's a lot of momentum toward an agile approach these days. And there sure are a lot of success stories of big companies that have made the transition to agile, such as Amazon and USAA, and more notably, Bosch, the

130-year-old German conglomerate.

There are, however, some negative aspects of older, entrenched companies that make adopting an agile approach difficult, and inflexibility is high on the list. Staying as fresh and agile as new start-ups is on every big business's minds these days … only it's hard to honor that when it takes the commitment, effort, introspection, and change we've seen over the preceding chapters. When a company prizes itself on its generations of tradition and organizational culture, it can be hard to upend that.

Like those lumbering tortoises, larger, older corporations are more risk averse. They're also often beholden to stakeholders in needing to show profit year over year. There's an ingrained bureaucracy, process, and structure that's tough to break through, and there's a monolithic structure when it comes to governance. Everything's so tightly wound together that altering a practice with one team will inevitably cause changes downstream with another and may even need buy-in from a third. After reaching a certain level of success, companies see different groups starting to pop up within their organization—the project managers, program managers, and portfolio managers—and they're all armed with status reports and project plans, becoming embedded seemingly everywhere. It's complicated to untangle.

Similar to those tortoises who plod along their same routine, companies that have been successful for years may not see the need to change. Heck, if it ain't broke, why fix it? It's hard for executives to understand why there's a reason to transform when it seems that they're not going to lose any customers by sticking with the status quo. Craig Larman's first law of organizational behavior highlights a truth of stasis with entrenched businesses: "Organizations are implicitly optimized to avoid changing the status quo middle- and first-level manager and "specialist" positions & power structures."[41] Essentially, bureaucracies crave middle management and vice-versa. There's a complexity that makes change both scary and unnavigable. The comfort for executives is the continued profit year after year; the comfort for the middle managers is the safety of the same job and no heavy lifting. Why would anybody make waves?

Well, you could probably ask Kodak executives whether, in retrospect, they should have enacted a groundbreaking change within their business.[42] By the time they finally realized that their core business was facing a dwindling customer base, they had already been disrupted out of the industry: fewer people were buying film and photographic elements, and more were buying digital hardware.

In fact, there are a number of large companies that have succeeded in shaking off the status quo and transitioning to an agile approach.

The Swedish telecommunications giant Ericsson started in 1876 as a telegraph repair shop before moving on to telephones a few years later, and now has a tremendous international footprint, controlling around a third of the global mobile infrastructure market. By the end of the 1990s, the company recognized that increased competition and the rapidity and convenience of intranet-based collaboration meant that it would have to find a new way of working to incorporate internal communications and refocus on the customer.[43] The company was building systems in five-year increments, and that clearly wouldn't satisfy customer demand. Ericsson began an agile transformation in 2011, and within a few years, the company was

---

41 Craig Larman, "Larman's Laws of Organizational Behavior," accessed November 22, 2018, https://www.craiglarman.com/wiki/index. php?title=Larman%27s_Laws_of_Organizational_Behavior.

42 Or ask the five now-extinct Galapagos tortoise species, laid to waste by merchants, whalers, and pirates who hunted for easy, long-lasting meat on ocean voyages from the seventeenth to nineteenth centuries!

43 Steve Denning, "Can Big Organizations Be Agile?" *Forbes*, November 26, 2016, accessed November 21, 2018, https://www.forbes.com/sites/stevedenning/2016/11/26/can-big-organizations-be-agile/#869ff9938e79.

working on deployments in three-week iterations. According to one product development manager's perspective, there were three things helping lead this highly successful transition: leadership fully embracing and training in agility, an autonomous and self-organized group of agile coaches within the organization, and constant retrospectives for evaluation and correction. All of these, in different ways, helped change the mind-set and culture and has kept the transition on track.[44]

Another multinational company that recognized its need for agility and found great success in transforming is ING. The financial services corporation likewise traces its organizational roots back to the mid-nineteenth century and has numerous subsidiaries, entrenched governance processes, and complicated structures. Former COO Bart Schlatmann cited no real financial imperative to spur on its recent agile transformation but noted that the company was already glimpsing change in customer behavior to trend toward more digital offerings.

Schlatmann recognized the key message in all agile transformations and the reason for knowing yourself: agile itself isn't an end but, rather, a *means* to that end, whatever your company's broad objective is. The ING leadership team realized that the company needed to "provide a seamless and consistently high-quality service so that customers can start their journey through one channel and continue it through another."[45] Furthermore, Schlatmann saw one other point I want to highlight: All companies, ING being no different, are technology companies. In the case of ING, it was a tech company operating as a financial services one.

---

44   Hendrik Esser, and Ben Linders, "Agile Transformation at Ericsson," *InfoQueue, blog,* September 10, 2018, accessed November 19, 2018, https://www.infoq.com/articles/agile-transformation-ericsson.

45   "ING's Agile Transformation," *McKinsey Quarterly.* January 2017, accessed November 20, 2018, https://www.mckinsey.com/industries/financial-services/our-insights/ings-agile-transformation.

In 2015, ING began a contained agile pilot program: "just" the 3,500 people at headquarters in the various departments, such as operations and technology development, marketing, and product management. Over the course of the year, by instilling and reinforcing the culture/mind-set change of "ownership, empowerment, customer centricity," by holding training sessions and offsites, building the right teams, reconfiguring spaces to allow for more face-to-face interaction, holding less formal meetings, and adapting to dev ops cross-functional teams and CI/CD, ING had instituted the agile approach across all of central headquarters. [46]

ING's CIO Peter Jacobs listed four major ingredients in the agile transformation, all of which may sound familiar by now: sitting operations and technology and the business together for constant communication; clarifying roles; establishing continuous delivery in two-week iterations; and breaking the old-school management role, and instead, focusing on *how* people use "knowledge."[47]

How large companies approach agile transformations are unique, as are the ways they ensure they succeed. When a John Deere software engineer wanted to expand agile to the farm equipment company's R&D groups, he began publishing articles about agile practices and created an agile conversation group on the company's internal social networking board.[48]

However, there are certain things I've found useful for large organizations to focus on to ensure a transformation takes hold.

---

46   Ibid.

47   "ING's Agile Transformation," *McKinsey Quarterly.* January 2017, accessed November 20, 2018, https://www.mckinsey.com/industries/financial-services/our-insights/ings-agile-transformation.

48   Darrell K. Rigby, Jeff Sutherland, and Hirotaka Takeuchi, "Embracing Agile," *Harvard Business Review,* May 2016, accessed November 21, 2018, https://hbr.org/2016/05/embracing-agile.

SMALL BATCH SIZES

If you have in place the proper tools that we discussed in the last chapter, and your CI/CD pipeline is optimized for low transaction costs for deployments, thanks to a highly efficient automated workflow, small batch sizes is one of the most important things you should be focusing on.

Why? Let's examine this fun and informative learning tool that I and other agile coaches use called the penny game.[49] You create groups of five people, and hand each group ten coins. One of the five team members is the timekeeper, and the others have to "process" the coins by flipping them over and handing them off to the next person. The timekeeper starts the clock when the first person turns the first penny and ends the clock when the last person flips the last.

In one iteration, the first person has to flip them all over one at a time before handing the entire ten-coin batch over to the second person, who does the same, and so on, all the way down the line. In another iteration, as soon as the first person flips a penny, she hands it off to the second person. As the second person is flipping that first coin over, the first person is flipping the second to pass off, and they keep moving the coins down the line simultaneously.

As you've probably guessed, this is a demonstration of large batch sizes versus small batch sizes. What the timekeeper will observe and relay is that the small batch of one item at a time progressing through the system is invariably quicker than the large batch of ten items. No

---

49   There are many modified versions of this, but this is the format that I generally use with my teams.

matter how quickly each individual can flip ten coins before handing them off, the small batch size always wins.

The proof of smaller batch sizes reducing cycle time comes from Little's theory of the law of queuing, which is, basically, the study of waiting in lines and is a lot more interesting than it sounds. The law posits that, assuming a standard processing rate, as you decrease line length for a service, waiting for that service also decreases. Sounds simple, sure. And yet it was somewhat groundbreaking in the mid-twentieth century, and large companies still haven't internalized what that actually means for their development pipeline. The law also suggests that as wait decreases, so, too, does delay and waste, while flow and predictability of outcome increases. Another ancillary benefit of the small batch size route along with the swifter, more efficient group operation is that there's less idle worker time.

Start-ups are extraordinarily good at deploying things in small batches, a concept that comes from lean manufacturing and development principles. As the penny game shows, small batches flow through the system faster. Meanwhile, large companies focusing on one or two deployments a year have no choice but to throw everything and the kitchen sink into them. Putting three hundred initiatives into a system in a big-bang type of deployment can be costly and time-consuming and carry with it a ton of variability.

There's quicker feedback with smaller batch sizes. Because it takes longer for large batches to run through to production, there's a longer wait time to get the rundown of mistakes and fixes to be implemented. With small batches, it's a narrower frame for where an error could occur. You'll be able to locate errors more quickly, prioritize which ones need attending to more quickly, and adjust for optimization piece by piece, building a better product along the way. Small batch sizes also offer greater visibility and transparency, something that's especially important for locating where bottlenecks are in the process and dealing with them.

Risk reduction is another benefit. Larger batch sizes bring with them a greater possibility of an error somewhere in the code or a feature. They also bear a higher chance of scheduling delays as well as higher expenses. Smaller batches, on the other hand, reduce the complexity and lessen the chance that anything—time frame, cost, or scope—gets off track. Or if they do, it's much easier to do a root-cause analysis and locate the errors with smaller batches.

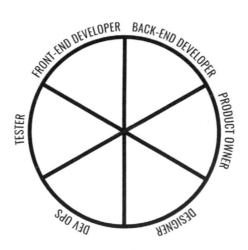

CROSS-FUNCTIONAL TEAMS

A common attribute in large companies is the preponderance of siloed teams: product in one organizational group, marketing in another, technology in another. It's routine with banks, where you have functional areas that report to each C-level executive (e.g., product teams reporting to the chief product officer). Small start-ups don't adhere to that model, though often that's because they just don't have the manpower. But guess what? Neither do some large companies, such as Microsoft and Amazon, because they've found the power of cross-functional teams ... and it seems to come straight out of dolphins' playbooks.

Instead of a permanent structure, dolphins' social networks are accessible and flat. They're able to move in and out of pods at will, a testament to their advanced intelligence. And what can bind the dolphins to one another can be anything from familial relations to similar age to simply mutual liking. There are certain advantages to joining new pods: better access to food, a different path through the ocean, stronger defense against predators.

There are a number of benefits to cross-pollinating between different jobs, making sure each unit has all of the various functions, such as testing, engineering, and business. As Eric Ries maintains, "Cross-training sometimes yields unexpected results."[50] Getting disparate departments in a room together to create a super squad generally aids creativity and innovation. There's no better way to out-side-the-box problem solving than having different minds working on a problem from different vantage points. With members of other disciplines operating together, cross-functional teams also reduce lags and bottlenecks that emerge from waiting for another department's skill set. Likewise, cross-functional teams communicate more quickly and more effectively, as the members representing different job skills have context for the conversation and don't need the scheduling of major departmental meetings.

The ownership of the product that comes from an autonomous team with few dependencies also should not be overlooked. With more independent authority and transparency in the process, the team members are naturally more invested in the outcome and will feel the impact their own work has had on the product. Successes will

---

50   Eric Ries, *The Startup Way*, New York: Currency, 2017, p. 68.

boost morale, and failures will impel members to take responsibility more readily.

Perhaps most importantly, instead of focusing solely on their own component in the stop on the old assembly line, each team is now concentrating on the end product and the customer's experience. Everything comes back to the value of the final product release and fulfilling the end user's satisfaction.

The end result of an innovative and collaborative team trusting each other, working in tandem on various aspects of the product, and communicating well about roadblocks, leads to faster delivery. This, in turn, brings in feedback sooner, and an optimized product sent to market more quickly.

For an operations and technology director at C. H. Robinson, the logistics and transportation company, part of the success of the company's agile transformation was due to this change in composition: "We made changes by creating smaller cross-functional teams that could deliver value with minimal cross-team dependencies. We went from an average of eighteen teams needed to accomplish milestones to cross-functional teams that were able to deliver something of value without complex dependencies. We are now consistently delivering value to our branch offices and our customers on a regular basis versus a multiyear timeline. We went from quarterly releases to releases each day."[51]

As for team size, larger companies may not be able to immediately create these cross-functional supersquads of just eight or nine people. They may have to start with a large chunk such as forty or fifty, the sort of team of teams that SAFe prescribes. Eventually, they may see their teams able to work their way down in numbers. As Jeff

---

51   Steve Denning, "Can Big Organizations Be Agile?" *Forbes*, November 26, 2016, accessed November 21, 2018, https://www.forbes.com/sites/stevedenning/2016/11/26/can-big-organizations-be-agile/#869ff9938e79.

Bezos famously made clear with his two-pizza rule (you should never have a meeting where two pizzas couldn't feed the entire group), small teams are nimble and agile. Again, every company is different. There's no magic number for teams per se, but companies ought to have an eye on making each team semiautonomous and reducing dependencies.

Less is more in so many different ways within an agile company.

Less is more in so many different ways within an agile company. Having four hundred software engineers paid on an hourly basis and spread out in three different cities may look appealing from a financial statement perspective, but when it comes to value delivery, quality, and speed, that model is broken. Let me air this one heretical notion: if a company practicing this were to ask me to come in as a coach, I'd propose getting rid of those 400 hourly employees, using the money to hire fifty high-end engineers, and colocating them in one city. Within a year, I guarantee, they'd be producing as much if not more in innovation and output as that four-hundred-engineer sprawl.

GIVE THEM TIME TO INNOVATE

Reading Google's "Nine Principles of Innovation" is like reading an agile handbook of best practices: "focus on the user," "ship and iterate," and "have a mission that matters." Two of them speak directly to employee empowerment and creativity: "innovation comes from anywhere" and "give employees 20 percent time." Allowing your business's women and men the time to pursue projects that unleash a spark, and *also* recognizing that ingenuity for any path can come from anywhere within the company make employees feel significantly valued at a company.

A great work environment is more than just a sizable paycheck or great cafeteria. Allotting your workers the space to think big, take risks, and fail helps the overall happiness substantially. When failure after a big, bold idea is punished, or when an employee's imaginative enterprise isn't properly valued, it can lead to demoralization and stifled creativity.

> **Real innovation is never going to happen if your employees aren't empowered to think creatively on their own.**

Eric Ries talks about the hockey stick curve, and how middle managers have learned to exploit companies' risk-averse nature. He avers that these people are incentivized to keep their teams on the flat part of the hockey stick long enough to earn a promotion.[52] Essentially, they're being rewarded for not taking any risks and aiming for a middling mediocrity, before growth reaches that inflection point to go dramatically up (or down). So ultimately, many big, staid businesses are telling their employees to keep their heads down and not think too far outside the box. Just play by the rules.

Real innovation is never going to happen if your employees aren't empowered to think creatively on their own. And it could very well make for an uninspired office at which average effort is the norm.

---

52   Khe Hy, "Lean Startup Evangelist Eric Ries on How Big Companies Can Stay Competitive," *Quartz*, December 6, 2017, accessed November 23, 2018, https://qz.com/work/1132506/lean-startup-evangelist-eric-ries-on-how-big-companies-can-stay-competitive/.

Investing in imaginative employees, giving them license to fail with strong ideas unleashes energy and can be infectious.

Google's 20 percent time for their employees, or Atlassian's twenty-four-hour hackathon are excellent examples of companies properly investing in their workers, leading to greater happiness and productivity. If those companies can spare the time in their schedules for this, others can as well.

BE CUSTOMER FOCUSED

Jeff Bezos famously calls every day "day one" at Amazon. Of his four pillars of success, "customer focus is by far the most protective of Day 1 vitality."[53] For any company striving to stay nimble and agile, starting with the customer should be of tantamount concern. It's the first of the twelve agile principles: "Our highest priority is to satisfy the customer through early and continuous delivery of valuable software."

Amazon's most profitable arm in its enterprise is Amazon Web Services, providing infrastructure-as-a-service, a far cry from its humble mid-90s beginnings as an online e-tailer of books. One thing the company and Bezos has continually done over its quarter century is stay fresh, modern, relevant, and forward thinking—agile. After five years of utilizing agile-type practices in its business, Amazon began transforming to adopt scrum in its software engineering departments

---

53   Jeff Bezos, "Amazon Letter to Shareholders," 2016, https://www.sec.gov/Archives/edgar/data/1018724/000119312517120198/d373368dex991.htm.

in the mid-2000s.

As Bezos explained in his 2016 letter to the shareholders, "Staying in Day 1 requires you to experiment patiently, accept failures, plant seeds, protect saplings, and double down when you see customer delight. A customer-obsessed culture best creates the conditions where all of that can happen."

Agile recognizes that the customer knows what she wants better than the in-house subject matter expert analyst; it's why that role is converted to product management and product ownership, and why the responsibility moves from documentation to seeking consistent feedback and input from the customer. This is a study in how agile values end users speaking for themselves.

> **Large companies immersed in waterfall are so concerned about business process mapping that the "customer" isn't even a consideration.**

Large companies immersed in waterfall are so concerned about business process mapping that the "customer" isn't even a consideration. They're focused on the different internal steps moving a product from idea to deployment, without ever checking in with the end user to gauge reception. Too often, the people involved with the systems and processes are building them based on their own biases and expertise. Your company isn't creating the feature or product for your own employees. You're building it for the customer.

It's important for your organization to map internal business processes, but remember that the customer journey map is arguably *more* important, especially for large companies. Customer journey mapping, some sort of representation of how users or clients engage with the product and company from start to finish, is essential in a

customer-obsessed agile world. In fact, sometimes that overall experience can be as highly regarded as the product itself: "Winning brands
owe their success not just to the quality and value of what they sell,
but to the superiority of the journeys they create."[54]

You want to feel like a start-up? Talk to your customers and
focus on satisfying them, not your PMs.

HIRE MIDDLE INFIELDERS

It's not dolphins and tortoises, but the philosopher Isaiah Berlin had
a semiserious notion of categorizing people as animals: He used foxes
and hedgehogs, a notion sifted down through the years, starting
with a Greek philosopher. The gist is that a hedgehog knows one
thing *extremely* well, and views everything through that lens. The
fox pursues a wide variety of ideas, and uses that to inform his world
view. While you may want to hire a hedgehog to pursue one giant
idea with an overarching vision, having foxes on your team can help
deliver various and unorthodox strategies for different problems.

Using another analogy: middle infielders are athletic enough
to move around the field. Fill a team with shortstops and second
basemen, and you'll be able to slot them in at any position and they'll
figure it out based on their innate athleticism. Not so with lumbering
first basemen or bulky catchers.

---

54   David C. Edelman, and Mark Singer, "Competing on Customer Journeys," *Harvard Business Review*, November 2015, p. 100, accessed March 6, 2019, https://hbr.org/2015/11/competing-on-customer-journeys.

Hire middle infielders. Instead of a corner outfielder who's gotten really good at his craft of manning right field and developing a strong throwing arm, middle infielders can fill any position you need them at if given a little time to figure it out. Start-ups can go overboard on this a bit and prize versatility in all areas when sometimes they actually need specific expertise. There are certainly areas where you'll need that specialization. But "middle infielders" are the problem solvers and collaborators; they're the ones that have the right DNA and behavior attributes to figure it out, be team players, and shift where the group most needs intelligence.

Many large companies have successfully transitioned to agile, implementing their own practices that are unique to where they are in their own stage of growth. Saab, Phillips, GE, Cisco, AT&T, and 3M are just some of the myriad corporations that have found success in transitioning part of if not all of their company to an agile approach. One thing to remember is that companies that have shown success in this arena continue to assess their agile mind-sets. As Steve Denning writes, "All of these firms are on journeys. None of them have arrived. None of them present themselves as having 'the solution.' None of them see Agile as a panacea. All of them are facing challenges, even the most famous of them. That can be a reassurance to firms that are earlier in their own journey."[55]

Every business is different, and every journey will be as well. Out-of-the-box "Agile!" paint-by-the-number kits won't work, nor will maintaining your agile approach without evaluation and upkeep as you grow.

Large companies are constrained by a number of factors: multiple layers of management, siloed departments that host unwieldy

55 Steve Denning, "Can Big Organizations Be Agile?" *Forbes*, November 26, 2016, accessed November 21, 2018, https://www.forbes.com/sites/stevedenning/2016/11/26/can-big-organizations-be-agile/#869ff9938e79.

meetings, demanding shareholders, risk aversion, and, frankly, comfort. If they've come this far, why change? Clearly something is going pretty well. Though you know better than that. You know that continually advancing technology and changing customer needs will never allow the ground beneath your organization to remain stable. The practices mentioned above can help your big business operate as a small start-up does, and in-house agile champions will help keep your company honest when it comes to upholding the agile principles and manifesto.

Start-ups may be inherently more agile and innovative than large, slower companies weighed down by tradition and bureaucracy. But if these big businesses are able to recapture some of that start-up energy *and* bring their established capital to the table, they can become powerful and nimble, combining the best of both worlds.

Chapter 13

HOW AGILE CAN WORK FOR YOU ... DESPITE EVERYTHING YOU'VE BEEN THROUGH

It can be difficult to recover when relationships fail. After two partners devote so much time and energy to strengthening their bond, in hopes of a long-lasting connection, for some reason, things fall apart. Maybe one partner leaves with a broken heart; maybe the other can't help but obsess over what he or she should have done to work it out. Both partners swear they'll never trust another person, and all they're left with is baggage and bad memories. Broken agile implementations are not so dire that you wolf down a pint of ice cream and listen to sentimental love tracks while burning old pictures, but they *can* leave companies wounded, also swearing they'll never go down that path again.

As with romantic relationships gone awry, failed agile experiences shouldn't sour you on the possibility of finding a good match in the future. Broken hearts can heal, and broken implementations can be mended. They can be hard to bounce back from, but if you think about what you want, take the time to know yourself and what you need, and remain steadfast and committed, you can redouble your efforts at a second shot.

Do you believe your people are your most important asset, and that your customer should be your most important focus? If you truly value these ideas and care about the quality of your software, you owe it to your business to consider the agile approach again. Remember that you don't need to be Spotify to make it work. You don't need to be a market leader, such as Google or Amazon, with money to burn. Nor do you have to be a small start-up working out of a two-bedroom rental. You don't need to be a company with a visionary leader who has revolutionary ideas to implement agile, or one in a unique situation with already-existing techniques and levers in place.

The approach is simpler than that. It's knowing who you are, what you want to accomplish, a legitimate dedication from all sides, and a discipline to see it through. Nothing fancy, just that commitment to making it work. Be honest with yourself. Will undergoing this holistic change—in culture, mind-set, personnel, and technical process, and a potential dip in short-term productivity—work for your company, considering your needs? Can your organization embrace fear and the unknown and not get in the way of itself?

Fear of the new and the complex is understandable. An agile approach, however? It's pretty simple. Of course, there's a distinction between easy and simple. It's simple to get well-defined muscles: go to the gym every day. But it's certainly not easy. Nor is a transformation to agile. However, it is *simple*, and the results are undeniable. The path itself takes time to work through, but the steps themselves are simple as long as you know where you're putting your feet.

The most important underlying step in all of this is to know yourself. It's the key to figuring out if agile is the right step for you to take; it's the main ingredient in uncovering what's unique about your company and how to implement agile in a way that will afford you the best chance of success. All of the other steps fit into this: how to adjust and adapt based on deeply understanding your company and its people. See the Appendix for a complete and concise step-by-step guide.

> **The most important underlying step in all of this is to know yourself. It's the key to figuring out if agile is the right step for you to take.**

Think about what we've discussed over the course of the book:

- *Your initial diagnostic.* In the beginning, we looked at what your introspective evaluation should cover—an objective look at your company to see your business, your people, and your processes for what they are, separately and as a whole.

  The first step is asking the right questions in a dialogue with staff. Don't enter into these conversations with an agenda to prove a hypothesis about what you believe your company can benefit from. This was my downfall early in my career, coming to an open conversation to better understand a company but carrying a lot of confirmation bias. That's not effective for a consultant, and it's a bad approach for a company looking to figure out its next steps.

Every company is different. Ask the right questions and keep yourself open to what the reviews and internal dialogue will uncover. Talk with everyone. Staffers from all levels will have valuable input. As Google proselytizes, innovation can come from anywhere. When you collect and synthesize all of the answers, consider the big question: is it worth it *for your company and what you want to accomplish* to undergo this transformation to agile? If so, what needs to change to make this happen?

- *Understanding the actual principles.* With so much misinformation about agile out there, prevailing myths endure and scare executives off. Similarly, shallow comprehension of it would have some believe that all company transformations are the same. Not so. Learn the actual foundations of what agile is, and why agile has to be tailored to each organization.

  This is a language that you, your consultant, and whoever ends up being your internal champions within the company will need to be fluent in. Because an agile transformation will ask a lot of your business in cost, time, and effort, buy-in is essential from all departments and people, top-down. Leadership will have to know what's fully required of them and that it's not enough to write a check, but that they'll have to be an active participant in the transition. Every part of your company should understand that agile is not only for the engineers; it's a change that will affect every department, from software engineering to accounting to marketing to human resources.

- *Training for the new world.* Once disparate divisions are on the same page, training for new roles and education for existing departments is a must: clarifying whose role is whose; how management will move from micromanaging to leading, inspiring, and facilitating; and how the expectations of each position will change. How are analysts going to transition from being the subject matter expert to being a customer-centric PO more interested in acquiring feedback than offering solutions? How will finance adjust to software releases in iterative deployments?

  Through training, you'll be able to figure out who your organization's all-stars and internal champions are. The people near the software engineering process can help lead your transition. They're the core transformation team, the ones to be meeting with regularly and to be entrusted with this responsibility. On the opposite side, you'll also be able to figure out who's *not* going to work in your new world of agile. Those who want to get it all done by themselves may have an undeniable value add, but if they can't work as collaborators and bristle at what's newly required of them, it may be time for them to move on.

- *The role of culture.* This cannot be underestimated. The only way an agile transformation can take hold and stick is if the culture of the company is conducive for such a change. Make sure your company values are congruous and upheld throughout every department. That happens from the top down. Leadership learns how to trust others and let go.

Siloed departments are broken up into autonomous cross-functional teams. Managers turn into servant leaders.

Incentivize employees with rewards beyond a paycheck. Actually value them as part of the company, trust them to come up with solutions, and grant them the freedom to fail. Allow them to grow within the company, and show how they're part of something bigger than their solitary task. This lack of command-and-control hierarchy may be scary to middle managers trained in just that, and they may take opportunities to instigate their own authority. That's going to be a bad fit for an agile business.

- *Looking at new data.* As the company and its people are viewed through a different lens, there are also new data points to tell the story of your software engineering. Which KPIs are worth tracking, based on the qualities you want to improve? There are metrics devoted to assessing predictability, lead time, defect trends (and many other aspects) that you may never have used. Also figure out what your current baseline is. You'll need to know where you're starting from if you want to do better. The KPIs will tell the full story of your workflow and further help your internal investigations of who you are. Onboard your people onto one centralized tracking tool, and encourage the face-to-face interactions that are part of the foundation of agile.

- *Getting to small batches and a CI/CD pipeline.* The new metrics are part of the overall change in how an agile company enacts a new software engineering workflow. It attends to lean principles and is based on what *The Lean*

Startup author Eric Ries named the minimum viable product (MVP). If your customers are the most important thing, getting their feedback is paramount in perfecting the product. The waterfall approach was a heavy, linear process of upfront documentation and analysts creating BRDs and FRDs. Agile puts the engineers in a cross-functional team with other skill sets in the room to minimize roadblocks and have quick turnaround. They're tasked with creating an MVP, putting it into production, getting feedback, and adjusting accordingly. This happens with the small batch philosophy, the idea that instead of months of work for patches or products that will involve a ton of changes, bite-sized pieces can reach the market and realize value more quickly.

It's simple. It's not easy, but it's simple. And it's worth it. When you look at all of these steps together, the underlying theme becomes clear: agile can work for you if you truly know who your company is, and how the approach should be tailored for your distinct enterprise, situation, and people. Self-awareness builds a stronger organization.

> ## Self-awareness builds a stronger organization.

Every company is unique. There's no out-of-the-box solution for which of *your* managers should fit where, or which automation tool is right for *your* engineers. You can't copy and paste the process from another company, even if it's roughly your size, is in the same industry, and has roughly the same amount of business or market cap. Imitating another company's best practices could leave yours with another broken relationship and wounded heart. Know yourself, and take a holistic approach to metamorphosing your company in simple steps.

Remember that the journey is never done. Your company won't be the same in two years as it is today. Having in-house champions to ensure you're adhering to the agile manifesto and the twelve agile principles, as you grow, is crucial. As you expand, and as you reach new inflection points, don't follow the instructions set forth from a consultant or from what worked last time. Reassess. If necessary, start from the beginning with a new internal diagnostic. It's the simplest, if not the easiest, way of making sure agile is working for you.

The power that comes when you know yourself has been written about by the Ancient Greek and Chinese Taoist thinkers alike. It's inscribed on the Temple of Apollo at Delphi, even if they weren't quite thinking about software engineering. But it applies to business practices as well as philosophical introspection with the same goal of attaining a clear vision. Understanding what you're looking for, how you want to achieve it, and what will and won't work can position your company to enact major changes effectively. After what I prescribe as a holistic approach to transforming from the inside out, you'll arrive at that end goal: delivering value faster with higher quality and more predictability to your customer base.

Conclusion

As fate would have it, while I was writing this book, a small, saltwater reef fish called the cleaner wrasse became the latest species to pass the mirror test. According to researchers, this shouldn't have been a surprise: "The cleaner wrasse has a great memory capacity, great cognitive capacity, and their social dynamics are pretty incredible."[56]

So maybe self-awareness is trending these days. The cleaner wrasse would join dolphins, bonobos, orangutans, orcas, Asian elephants, magpies, and a few other animals who've passed the mirror test and know themselves.

The mirror test was conceived in 1970, and though there are other ways we may be able to assess whether an animal is self-aware, it's been the industry standard since then. In the test, an animal is marked with a dot, sticker, or paint somewhere on its body it can't normally see. It's then shown a mirror. If the animal investigates or interacts in any way with the mark on its own body, it recognizes that the creature it's looking at in the mirror is its own self.

Why is this so important? How does recognizing one's reflection

---

56   Ryan F. Mandelbaum, "A Fish Just Passed a Mirror Test for Self-Awareness, but What Does That Mean?" *Gizmodo*, February 7, 2019, accessed February 8, 2019, https://gizmodo.com/a-fish-just-passed-a-mirror-test-for-self-awareness-bu-1832430572.

become a mark of internal self-awareness, and what the heck did any of this have to do with agile transformations?

Think about looking at yourself in a mirror. When you see your own reflection, you're able to self-critique, and then change something about yourself. Even if it's as simple as getting a blue sticker off your face, you can improve and change your perspective.

Take it a step further. Upon seeing your reflection in the mirror, you get instant feedback about an action you take: what you look like baring your teeth or rolling your eyes. Watching yourself leads you to consider how those actions may play in a social setting and can help you regulate your emotions. This helps you think about a larger group setting and your role in it. Other theories about the mirror test go even deeper. One supports the idea that self-awareness via the mirror test measures problem-solving ability.[57]

Essentially, having access to a mirror and investigating your own reflection leads to an awareness that allows you to self-inspect, adapt, improve, work more functionally in a group setting, and solve problems. Or as the researcher noted about the cleaner wrasse, capitalize on great cognitive capacity and social dynamics.

If that's not agile, I don't know what is.

The two animals I set up as counterpoints for this book, a dolphin and tortoise, represent for me two opposite sides of a spectrum for businesses. Slow-moving, impenetrable, and ancient, tortoises clearly have a lot in common with organizations that are slow to transform and likely to burrow in and double down on whatever has worked in the past. The speedy, agile, and fun-loving dolphins epitomize to me the flexible companies that have looked in the mirror, taken stock of what they see, and said, "Yeah, we could improve all this."

The self-awareness that may progress to better social interaction

---

57   Michael D. Breed, and Janice Moore, "Cognition," in *Animal Behavior,* New York: Elsevier, 2012, p. 151–182, https://www.sciencedirect.com/science/article/pii/B9780123725813000064?via%3Dihub.

is becoming more and more apparent in dolphins. In 2016, researchers at a Ukrainian nature reserve recorded two dolphins having a conversation in standard talk and response, in which each would click and pulse in response to the other without interrupting. Also in 2016, scientists in Florida published a paper proving that dolphin communication increases as they tackle more complicated tasks, as if they were attempting to solve a problem.[58]

It's these kinds of social and business implications of self-awareness that speak directly to what it takes to undergo or fix an agile implementation. Reflecting on what we see and then diving deeper to understand what it means to be part of a group is at the core here. An agile transformation will be successful if there's strength and trust in the team: everyone in the organization in the same mind-set on what agile is seeking to accomplish, all part of a congruous culture that's initiated from top-down, cognizant that the company is its own unique self, and each team member is integral to the process, ready to take on new roles and responsibilities, able to work in cross-functional teams and communicate more and more with customers and other coworkers out from behind a screen.

These traits stem from that core ability and fearless inclination to, frankly, look in a mirror and recognize yourself. Take stock of where you are, and where you have to go if you want to improve. It seems fitting that scientific research is revealing that more and more animals are conscious and self-aware, just as businesses are recognizing the benefits of being the very same. Self-awareness is a gateway attribute that allows any kind of entity—animal or corporate—to take steps in advancement. At a certain point, animals of every sort are faced with that one final evolutionary credo: adapt or die.

---

58   Sarah Knapton, "Dolphins Recorded Having a Conversation 'just like Two People' for First Time," *Telegraph*, September 11, 2016, accessed February 7, 2019, https://www.telegraph.co.uk/science/2016/09/11/dolphins-recorded-having-a-conversation-for-first-time/.

Appendix

Agile Manifesto

We are uncovering better ways of developing
software by doing it and helping others do it.
Through this work we have come to value:

- **Individuals and interactions** over processes and tools

- **Working software** over comprehensive documentation

- **Customer collaboration** over contract negotiation

- **Responding to change** over following a plan

That is, while there is value in the items on
the right, we value the items on the left more.

The agile manifesto, conceived and written in 2001 by seventeen software practitioners, is the succinct summation of values for this engineering approach.[59] At its core, the manifesto is a set of four concepts to prioritize when working. Agile has moved far beyond just software engineering into many industries and organizations worldwide. Misconceptions and fly-by-night consultants are everywhere, as they are with any great and trendy idea, but I did my best throughout the book to clear away the confusion and create a roadmap for implementing—or fixing—agile within your business.

A few notes on the manifesto that I think are worth mentioning:

- In the first line of the manifesto, it's notable that the signers didn't say "uncovered," but rather "uncover*ing*," to denote the ongoing process. They recognized that they don't have all the answers, and what's true about agile today won't be true tomorrow. The process is always improving.

- Of the items valued more than others, my friend John Krewson succinctly notes that he'd pay more for the items on the left than those on the right. Not that processes and tools aren't important, but individuals and interactions are *more* important.

- The notion of customer collaboration addresses the fact that developing working software should be a dialogue with the user. With customer negotiation in the past, it was essentially a question of fighting with the customer to hammer out a contract, and then assign blame when the process or product wasn't up to snuff. Valuing collaboration

---

59   Agile Manifesto, "Manifesto for Agile Software Development," 2001, accessed December 28, 2018, http://agilemanifesto.org/.

means that the business is dedicated to building software *with* the customer instead of *for* the customer.

- Responding to change over following a plan puts your values in the right place. We protect what we value the most. If you're protecting the plan and the process instead of the ability to change, be flexible, and make a better product, then while it may be easier for you, your customers won't be satisfied.

The Twelve Principles of Agile

As was the manifesto, the twelve principles were written by the seventeen practitioners in 2001 and expand on the goals and values for the (then) young software engineering philosophy.[60] Below, I've added my own notes to each of the principles to help clarify or elaborate.

Our highest priority is to satisfy the customer through early and continuous delivery of valuable software.

This first principle is the biggest lesson for companies twisting themselves into knots to "implement agile." If you truly believe that the customer's right; if you believe that you don't know better than the customer in what she wants; if you believe that every step should be about delivering value to the customer and you commit to the processes and provisions in place to undertake it, you're already agile. You both believe and execute what agile wants you to implement. An agile approach looks to enter a collaborative relationship with the

---

60   "Principles behind the Agile Manifesto," agile manifesto, 2001, accessed December 28, 2018, http://agilemanifesto.org/principles.html.

customer and satisfy her by delivering quality software in a "good enough" draft to get feedback and improve the product on a continuous, iterative schedule.

Welcome changing requirements, even late in engineering. Agile processes harness change for the customer's competitive advantage.

The notion that requirements may change over the course of the product's development is heretical and flat-out scary for many software engineers, especially when it comes with the phrase "late in development." As a result, this is often where large companies and waterfall teams say, "Sorry. We can't afford to change large requirements. It would take too long."

Are we really saying that people can only have good ideas two or three times a year, and then they're cut off? Or is the *actual* problem with how the system is currently set up: the underlying infrastructure doesn't support changes, or the requirements document has too long a sign-off process, or any other number of traditional obstacles?

What if it *were* easy to make any of these changes just by pressing a button? What if there were multiple environments, and tasks could be automated? If these conditions were in place, there shouldn't be a software engineer in the world who would care about changing business needs.

So we welcome changing requirements, even if they're late in development because you know what? That's what happens. People have good ideas, throughout the world, throughout the year.

**Deliver working software frequently, from a
couple of weeks to a couple of months, with a
preference to the shorter timescale.**

This principle hammers home the point of continuous, iterative engineering. Software should be delivered to customers in small batches for easy troubleshooting and productivity, and quick feedback. Human beings are visual people. Let's see how they interact with it. Let's try doing small bites instead of these large chunks, and get the feedback to improve the product. Delivering often and frequently allows for a feedback loop, in which customers can tell you what's right, what's wrong, and what needs to be changed.

The small batch concept of delivering more frequently and in smaller chunks also helps with locating errors. In a waterfall process, it's only after nine months of analysis, requirement defining, design, and engineering that testing starts revealing mistakes. This forces engineers to go all the way back to the beginning. Because the product is so detailed and cascaded, they're forced to review everything to look for where the errors are located.

Agile sees value delivered every two weeks or so in smaller increments. Once an error is found, engineers don't need to go back to the beginning. Chances are it's in the latest set of functionality, making for easier identification and rectification.

**Business people and developers must work
together daily throughout the project.**

The wall between the business and software engineers has to come down. Instead of the old method of the business side establishing certain demands of software engineering at the beginning of the cycle, and then reappearing nine months later asking for their product, what if that relationship were different? What if the business were sitting side by side with software engineers, and both parties had the same goals and problem-solved together? What if they thought of themselves as a team?

In an us-versus-them mentality, product is concerned only with requirements, and software engineering only with implementation. But when product and software engineers have the same annual and quarterly goals, when it's both departments working with a shared goal in mind, then the organization is working in unity. Tear down that wall. Bring them together with a shared goal. Then this process is supported.

A simple, if not altogether easy solution, is to colocate the business and software engineers. Move your product people from Phoenix to Malaysia, where all your software engineers are. Or vice-versa. It may be impractical, but it would be a lot more efficient than hiring a bunch of scrum masters and agile coaches.

Build projects around motivated individuals.
Give them the environment and support they need,
and trust them to get the job done.

When you give your employees a supportive environment, trust, and autonomy, you empower them and improve morale significantly. Leaders in agile: you are no longer task masters. Your job is to inspire and remove obstacles. Let your employees shine. Be a coach. Give them the space to run things and the responsibility to do so. Motivate them to feel they're more than just employees. And more than anything, trust your team to make the right decisions. *That's* what being a leader is.

The most efficient and effective method of conveying information to and within a development team is face-to-face conversation.

No matter how advanced technology becomes, no matter how many ways we can avoid actually speaking to one another, the most effective way to convey information is by getting in a room and talking it out. So much communication can be nonverbal: how we respond to stimuli, how we receive information, whether or not we understand things can be gleaned not from our words, but from other clues. Wouldn't you want to see whether your team fully understands what you need to get done instead of relying on email for dialogue?

Instead of hiding behind electronic communications and PowerPoint presentations, have direct conversations with each other to answer questions and build toward the right solution.

Working software is the primary measure of progress.

"Percent complete" can officially go into the trash. The concept of finishing requirements and checking off the box that calls the project 10% done is gone. It never made sense: A product that was 95% done but had never spent time being tested in an active environment didn't make it just 5 percent away from completion. In an agile approach, you're at 0 percent done until a customer can actually use the software. Up until then, it's all academic.

Agile processes promote sustainable development. The sponsors, developers, and users should be able to maintain a constant pace indefinitely.

Whereas Toyota's lean manufacturing was all about making the process as efficient as possible, agile is interested in finding a sustainable pace that allows predictability. Can you replicate a pace over and over again? This also falls on leadership to have reasonable expectations on how much a team can deliver. Pushing a team to be faster with one specific deployment but never being able to duplicate that with any predictability harms the team and the user. Don't sacrifice predictability for speed.

Continuous attention to technical excellence and good design enhances agility.

The holistic, ground-up revolution in concept, personnel, and culture takes you very far in agile; but if you don't have the infrastructure in place that ensures best practices in software engineering, you won't realize the benefits. Having the architecture and framework in place will enable you, practically speaking, to have the mechanical tools and processes at your disposal to develop quickly, but you also need the culture of quality in place to ensure your engineers are committed to delivering high-quality software.

Simplicity—the art of maximizing the amount of work not done—is essential.

Less is more. This may be a very counterintuitive concept for businesses, but it's true. If you're focusing on too many tasks, you'll end up accomplishing less. If you have your software engineers focus on fifty different projects and a hundred different features, you'll lose efficiency. Make sure they focus on one piece or one area of functionality at a time. The simplicity of saying no helps with efficiency. Think about all of the buttons and functions in Word or Excel that the vast majority of users will never interact with, and all of the wasted time that went into developing them. This doesn't apply solely to the product but also to the process as well. Create, operate, and develop simply.

**The best architectures, requirements, and designs
emerge from self-organizing teams.**

Yes, there needs to be upfront design. There need to be foundations in place for software engineers from which to plan. But as opposed to the documentation-heavy, siloed architects defining the plans with no space for changes, agile mandates that room must be left for the teams themselves to adjust that architecture. This combines the trust and empowerment from the fifth principle. When motivated, self-organizing teams are given the proper environment and support, the best solutions emerge.

**At regular intervals, the team reflects on how
to become more effective, then tunes and adjusts
its behavior accordingly.**

The twelfth and final principle regards making a habit of reflecting and improving. This highlights the second and third pillars of the empirical process: inspection and adaptation.

Each methodology within agile uses, in one form or another, the three pillars of the empirical process: transparency, inspection, and adaptation. Scrum, the most widely used and known methodology, operates transparency by putting the requirements on cards that transform into user stories. Inspection then comes first with the iteration review, in which the business or PM / PO review and critique the software, and then with the iteration retrospective, in which the entire team reviews the process itself. Adaptation then happens as the team improves upon the process for the subsequent iteration.

The job is never done. You can always fine-tune and improve, grow a little smarter and create better practices. It's essential you do—not only in the middle of product development, not only in the middle of a year of growth or at its next inflection point—during deployments themselves. Just as each company is unique, your own company, at certain stages of growth, is unique. Always inspect and adapt.

A Step-by-Step Guide to Implementing Agile in Your Organization

☐ 1. **Perform a diagnostic** (chapter 3) on the current software development process, the organization, and the tools. Take an objective look at your company to see your business, your people, and your processes for what they are, separately and as a whole.

☐ 2. **Identify a transformation leader** (chapter 3) who understands software development and ideally has agile experience.

☐ 3. **Understand the principles**. Learn the actual foundations of what agile is and why agile has to be tailored to each organization. This enables companies to customize agile processes without violating the core tenets.

☐ 4. **Develop and conduct training** (chapter 3). Training for new roles and education for existing departments is a must: clarifying whose role is whose; how management will move from micromanaging to leading, inspiring, and facilitating; and how the expectations of each position will change. Training areas typically include:

- Agile specific
- Role based
- Tool
- Reporting / metrics
- Process focused
- Leadership oriented (servant leadership)

☐ 5. **Include other departments early** (chapter 3, chapter 6)—specifically finance and HR—this transformation isn't just focused on operations and technology. It will impact virtually every department in the company. Get buy-in early from other departments and explain what changes are in store for them.

☐ 6. **Pilot with a smaller group** (chapter 3). Identify a particularly strong and adaptable group on a much smaller scale and implement with that group. Learn from the pilot, adjust the processes accordingly, and roll out in an iterative approach across the company.

☐ 7. **Find champions** (chapter 3). Identify a small working group of individuals (staff and mid-level management) who can pick up the concepts early on, explain the principles, and proselytize to coworkers.

☐ 8. **Understand and communicate the why** (chapter 4). This drives the agile transformation roadmap and more importantly enables a company to obtain buy-in from all of the employees it impacts.

☐ **9.** **Assess current organization against new roles** (chapter 5). Any transformation brings change with it and more specifically changing roles. Assess how and where each team member fits against the new or modified roles.

☐ **10.** **Ensure a proper culture** (chapter 5, chapter 7) that supports a successful organization. Make sure your company values are congruous and upheld throughout every department. Work on instilling a culture that provides autonomy to individuals at all levels and a psychologically safe environment that embraces risk and sees failure as necessary for growth.

☐ **11.** **Define metrics and understand the baseline** (chapter 8). Identify what metrics you want to track and make sure you have the system (processes and governance), tools, and training in place to have accurate data.

☐ **12.** **Assess and upgrade the tools and infrastructure** (chapter 11). To fully reap the benefits of agile, ensure the infrastructure is designed and built to support CI/CD. This includes having automated tools in place, ensuring the CI/CD pipeline is effective and attended to, and committing to the DevOps practice.

☐ **13.** **Focus on small batch sizes** (chapter 12). This requires some attention to ensuring proper tools and infrastructure exist for CI/CD. It also requires an emphasis on a culture that values small batches and the need to train product to understand concepts like the Minimal Viable Product (MVP).

☐ **14.** **Identify opportunities for cross-functional teams** (chapter 12). Bring roles together from disparate departments, enabling more effective partnership and delivery.

☐ **15.** **Emphasize customer focus** (chapter 12). Talk to your customers and focus on satisfying their needs. Strive to understand their experience with your products and services and have that inform what the development teams should build.

☐ **16.** **Hire middle infielders** (chapter 12) that can fill multiple roles across an organization and excel at figuring things out given a little time, thus providing an organization with a lot of flexibility.

☐ **17.** **Continually reassess and course correct** (chapter 13). The agile transformation is never complete. Evaluate the progress and status of the transformation on a regular basis and adjust when needed.